Marriott®

Hot Shoppes

COOKBOOK

SIXTY YEARS OF AMERICAN COOKERY

Recipes tested, adapted, and supervised by Hot Shoppes:
Steven R. Leipsner, Executive Vice President and General Manager
Don Rodis, Vice President of Operations
Anne Hill, Director of Quality Assurance and Product Development
Arlette Schmitt-Constandy, Director of Food Standards
Sharon Thorpe, Project Manager
Keyvan Khayam, Project Assistant
Rosalie Aikens, Food Technologist
Deborah Sloan, Administrative Secretary
Keyvan Khayam, Project Assistant,

Creative Director/Editor	John Rose
Production Manager	Janie Mann
Art Director	Karl Bronk
Copywriter	Edward Nathan
Chief Photographer	Gale Frank-Adise
Photographer	David Doyle
Food Stylist	Robin Lutz
Prop Stylist	Nancy Lendved

Text, recipes, and photography copyright ©1987 Marriott Corporation

Library of Congress Cataloging-in-Publication Data

Marriott Hot Shoppes cookbook.

Includes index.
1. Cookery, American.   2. Marriott Hot Shoppes.
I. Marriott Hot Shoppes.   II. Marriott Corporation.
TX715.M36   1987   641.50973   87-25715
ISBN 0-9619257-0-1

Published in 1987 for Marriott Corporation by
Parsons, Friedmann, Stephan & Rose, Inc.
30 Newbury Street
Boston, MA 02116

Printed in Italy

To the memory of J. Willard Marriott, 1900-1985.
Founder of an American tradition in hospitality.

PREFACE

by J. W. Marriott, Jr.

As we conclude our sixtieth year of business, it's fitting that we consider the path that Marriott Corporation has followed to become a diversified, world leader in hospitality. It's been a long path, but also a direct one because we've held to the ideas of value and service embodied in the first restaurants my parents opened — the Hot Shoppes.

In many ways, the Hot Shoppes were a perfect setting for my father. They were family-style restaurants, which enabled him to interact warmly with both customers and co-workers. And since the earliest Hot Shoppes were all in the Washington, D.C. area, it was convenient for my father to inspect them regularly.

Those two activities, meeting customers and staff, and closely checking services and facilities, represent the essence of my father's idea of hospitality: courtesy and consistency, maintained through dynamic leadership. And that remains our philosophy at Marriott today.

While it is true that we have moved into many different areas over the years, as diverse as airline catering and life care facilities, all of these endeavors share the single goal of making people comfortable while they are away from their homes. Of course, we have far too many facilities for even a thousand Bill and Allie Marriott's to greet all of our guests at the door. But we have tried to instill in every one of our employees a commitment to the kind of personal warmth that has been my parents' gift.

Moreover, we have sustained our commitment to consistency, using many of the same techniques pioneered by my father. Where he employed recipe cards, and the weekly quizzing of his chefs and managers, we have implemented thorough training programs and the latest information technology. Still, the idea is the same, and the results are the same. Anyone who dines in a Marriott restaurant, or who sleeps under a Marriott roof, is assured of Marriott quality.

In offering you this collection of Hot Shoppes recipes, we are, in a sense, extending the Marriott standard of excellence even further...right into your own kitchen. Equally important, we want the *Marriott Hot Shoppes Cookbook* to mark our sixtieth anniversary. With this book we acknowledge our gratitude to those restaurants that established the high standards of hospitality to which we hold.

Bill Marriott, Jr.

TABLE OF CONTENTS

Preface by J.W. Marriott, Jr. i

Table of Contents iii

Acknowledgements iv

Introduction by Alice Sheets Marriott v

The Hot Shoppes Family Album 1

The Hot Shoppes Recipes 22

Beverages 24

Appetizers, Soups 30

Breads, Dressings 50

Sauces, Gravies 76

Salads, Salad Dressings 92

Sandwiches 112

Meats 122

Poultry 138

Casseroles 146

Fish, Seafood 156

Vegetables 170

Desserts, Dessert Sauces 184

Cakes, Frostings 200

Pies, Pastries 210

Directory of Hot Shoppes 224

Index 225

ACKNOWLEDGEMENTS

The Marriott Corporation wishes to express its gratitude to all the members of the Hot Shoppes family who have helped to maintain the enduring quality of the restaurants. The following friends and former employees were instrumental in retelling the history of the Hot Shoppes: Ambassador Mark Evans Austad, Martin Buxbaum, Fernand Coulon, Carolyn Holste, Robert Martin, Iva Savage, Helen Verstandig, J. Mack Woodward.

Special thanks to the following publishers:
"The Mad Reader" is © 1954 by E.C. Publications (appearing in "Sandwiches" section).
LIFE cover reprinted with permission. © 1969 TIME, Inc. (in "Vegetables" section).
SPIDER-MAN and the likeness thereof are Trademarks of the Marvel Entertainment Group, Inc. and are used with permission (in "Desserts, Dessert Sauces").
SUPERMAN is a trademark of DC Comics Inc., New York. Illustrations: Copyright © 1982 DC Comics Inc. Used with permission.
PEP and BETTY & VERONICA comics, logos, and character names and likenesses, TM and © 1969, ARCHIE COMIC Publications, Inc. (appearing in "Desserts, Dessert Sauces").
"At the Hop" sheet music © Singular Publishing, Inc. (appearing in "Fish, Seafood" section).

Marriott Corporation is grateful to the following individuals, shops, and organizations who also contributed their belongings, merchandise, and time to our photographic designs:

E.B. Adams (Washington, D.C.), The American Film Institute (Washington, D.C.), Appalachiana, Inc. (Bethesda, MD), A & W Root Beer (Atlanta, GA), Gertrude Berman (Monsey, N.Y.), Blue Moon (Washington, D.C.), Bobby Vee ("Walking with my Angel"), Brenda's Antiques & Collectibles (Washington, D.C.), Chenonceau Antiques (Washington, D.C.), Lisa Cherkasky (Washington, D.C.), Renee Comet Photography (Washington, D.C.), Georgetown Tobacco (Washington, D.C.), Peter Goodman (Chevy Chase, MD), David Graves (Washington, D.C.), Ira Grossman (Washington, D.C.), Hall China Company (E. Liverpool, OH), Hechinger Company (Bethesda, MD), Herman's World of Sporting Goods (Washington, D.C.), Johanna (Baltimore, MD), Dolly Kay Designs, Ltd. (Washington, D.C.), Kitchen Bazaar (Washington, D.C.), Tom Kochel (Washington, D.C.), John Ligon, Inc. (Bethesda, MD), Movie Madness (Washington, MD), National Zoological Park (Washington, D.C.), Adam Phillips (Washington, D.C.), Ruff and Ready Furnishings (Washington, D.C.), Uzzolo (Washington, D.C.), Williams-Sonoma (Washington, D.C.).

INTRODUCTION

by Alice Sheets Marriott

We've put together this cookbook to help you prepare the same popular dishes we've been serving in our restaurants since my husband and I opened the first Hot Shoppe in 1927. Or course, many dishes have been added over the years, and a few have been discontinued, but the selection here will give you a very good idea of the kinds of meals we've always served.

We're also hoping that our book will recreate the atmosphere of the Hot Shoppes and help you recall the meals you've enjoyed with us. And if you've never been to the Hot Shoppes, perhaps we can whet your appetite for these restaurants that have played a part in the lives of so many families.

That's why we've designed the *Marriott Hot Shoppes Cookbook* to resemble a family album. Our favorite slogan has always been "food for the whole family," and over the years we've delighted in sharing special occasions with the families of both employees and customers. Young men have proposed marriage in Hot Shoppes, children have grown up among us, senior citizens have enjoyed their retirements with us. The photos and memorabilia that we've included in our cookbook, together with the recipes, will help to preserve these memories.

But we're also looking ahead to sharing with new customers… creating new memories, so to speak. I hope that you'll welcome this book into your lives, and let us look over your shoulders while you're putting together a special dinner. As a dear friend once told me, "the Hot Shoppes are an extension of everyone's dining room." We want this cookbook to continue that tradition.

At the heart of that tradition is our commitment to making our customers feel comfortable. Indeed, welcoming guests to the Hot Shoppes was my late husband's greatest pleasure. If you were a regular diner at one of the Washington area Hot Shoppes in the earlier years, you are almost certain to have met him at one time or another—unless he was in the kitchen when you were visiting. He usually spent a great deal of time in the kitchen: inspecting, tasting, and encouraging our chefs, waitresses, and waiters, but never cooking (for someone who was so good at making precise judgements about recipes, Bill was never exactly at home behind a sauce pan).

But he knew what he liked, as do I, and that's what these recipes represent: a lifetime of traveling through America, dining with family and friends, discovering new tastes, or rediscovering old ones, and then working out the dishes for the Hot Shoppes. So it really is fair to call our cookbook "sixty years of American cookery." Though, to be completely accurate, you should know that not every recipe was learned in family settings: our Navy Bean Soup, for instance, is modeled after the famous soup served in the Senate Office Building. This soup had a distinctive quality Bill favored, and he supervised our chefs during the long period it took to capture that flavor.

In fact, Bill was always a stickler for detail. One reason we've been able to collect so many recipes is that he supervised the creation of Recipe Cards for every Hot Shoppes chef and cook, so that they would produce uniformly seasoned food. We've been able to use these cards in preparing recipes for the cookbook. In his spirit, I suggest that you try to follow these instructions exactly—just the way Bill insisted our chefs had to, when he conducted his famous inspections. Even so, I should also tell you that all of these recipes are the product of years of experimentation in our test kitchens, and years of sampling by our panel of taste experts (which included our radio spokesman Mark Evans, who insisted that he approve the dishes before he spoke about them to the public). If you feel you must experiment and tinker with the recipes, then in some way you're also honoring the Hot Shoppes tradition.

But the most important part of our continuing history will always be the family. That's probably why I usually think of the holiday seasons when I reminisce about the Hot Shoppes: we've shared so many festive occasions with so many people. Maybe it's because quite a few Hot Shoppes are in Washington, D.C., and because many people are called away from their families to do government work. So they need to find a social setting on the holidays. Or maybe it's just the warm feelings our employees have always had for each other and our guests. Whatever the reason, Hot Shoppes have always been warm and busy during those special seasons of the year.

Nothing would make me happier, than if some of the dishes in this cookbook would find their way to your holiday table.

Allie Marriott

Marriott®
The Hot Shoppes Family Album
Memories and Memorabilia

O ur scrapbook contains photographs real and remembered. The real pictures are, of course, snapshots of the changing Hot Shoppes through the years. The remembered pictures, however, are not real in the conventional sense: the particular scenes we're describing were never, to our knowledge, captured on film. But they're real in another sense, because they embrace and combine our most important memories. In the end, that's how we look at scrapbooks anyway—through a filter that selects and highlights the meaningful details of our lives. And to help explain the details and the meaning of these photos and memories, our Family Album also includes a brief history of the seven decades during which the Hot Shoppes have played a role in American lives.

I. *Window shopping for lunch— October 18, 1928*

Like the first snapshot in any treasured family album, our first remembered picture is old and fading. Perhaps the photographer didn't have it perfectly in focus. But we can still make out all the lettering on the large sign over the store front. On the upper left hand corner,

"Coffee, Sandwiches"; on the lower right corner, "Chili Con Carne, Hot Tamales"; and across the center, in large, flowing script letters, "The Hot Shoppe." Sunlight glints off the sign and the large plate glass window below it.

The front door of the shop is mostly obscured by the three men facing the store, their backs to the photographer—two in suits, one in workman's overalls, and all three are wearing hats, as was common in the earlier years of this century. They seem to be studying the activity inside the little restaurant.

A mustachioed man, in a tall, white chef's hat is standing inside the shop near the plate glass window. His posture is erect, as if his apron were as starched as his hat. A carving knife is clearly visible in his left hand, and on the cutting board in front of him there is a sandwich. From the tilt of the three spectator's heads, it's reasonable to assume that's what they're studying. The man at the left of the group is reaching for the elbow of the man in the middle, as if he is about to escort him into the restaurant.

To the right of the chef a long, large piece of meat, probably pork, is roasting on a spit. It's certainly possible that the three spectators are looking at this as well, and it's likely that the aroma of the barbeque first attracted the three men, since we can see wisps of smoke curling through the vent above the plate glass window.

The earliest Hot Shoppes
The Twenties

This first image comes pretty close to capturing those first few Hot Shoppes, built during the late Twenties. Of course, we also have a natural temptation to believe that this early picture somehow foreshadows the entire his-

tory of the Hot Shoppes: we like to assume that everything grows in a simple straight line. In the case of the Hot Shoppes, however, we can't make that

Original Hot Shoppe

T.W. Marriott & Robert Smire

assumption, because both America and the Hot Shoppes have changed and grown so unpredictably during the past sixty years.

Our early, faded snapshot, however, does reveal a few of the characteristics that became part of the Hot Shoppes legacy: clean places serving hot, sometimes spicy food, with just a dash of showmanship.

Let's begin with the name on the sign: "The Hot Shoppe." To understand how this simple name, with the stylized spelling, embodied Bill Marriott's plan for his restaurant,

we should take a brief look at the restaurant's predecessor, an A & W Root Beer franchise, which he opened in 1927 at 3128 Fourteenth Street NW in Washington, D.C. Considering the sizzle of the Washington summer, and the pricing—"Five cents for a frosty mug"—it was a good business. But because Marriott's agreement with A & W limited him to to serving only cold root beer, it was only a seasonal business, and Bill wanted to stay open year round. So he secured permission from Roy Allen of A & W to serve food that would warm Washington through the wet chill of an eastern winter. Hot food. And then he selected the simple name that would explain the special value of his food—"The Hot Shoppe." He didn't realize at the time that he

was going to be so successful that he would have to add an "s" to the end of the name within a few months, when he opened his second Hot Shoppes.

But what food, exactly, would he serve? Years earlier, as a rancher in the cold shadows of Utah's Wasatch Mountains, Bill had discovered the appetizing and thermal properties of chili peppers. Chili con carne, tamales, and barbeque had sustained Bill through his long vigils with his herd, and he guessed that they'd work just as well in Washington, D.C.—where the shepherds wore dark suits, and kept their sheepskin on the walls of their busy offices.

Only one problem remained—neither Bill nor his wife Alice knew how to prepare Mexican and southwestern

Connecticut Ave.

specialties. For this challenge, Washington, D.C. provided a better solution than even Utah or Arizona: the Mexican Embassy. Alice Marriott spoke Spanish fluently, and made so good an impression on the embassy chef that he not only provided her with a sheaf of recipes, but also gave the Marriotts access to his Texas supplier for the more exotic ingredients. Remember, before the days of large supermarkets with gourmet departments, finding cumin seed, or chili peppers was a formidable task. Southwestern cuisine may have been a good idea for Washington, but it was not going to be the most convenient.

The final touch was the carving chef, who is so prominent in our photograph. Bill brought him down from New York, and he quickly became a spectator attraction. To complement his performance, the rotisserie was

carefully positioned under a fan and vented to send out aromatic enticements. During the Depression, in fact, down-and-out residents of Washington's Ninth Street often

gathered in such numbers that they blocked the sidewalk around the second Hot Shoppes. Bill Marriott offered them food for work.

Bill also had paying customers, however. A lot of them. His prices were low, even for the Depression, the menu was unique, the service was courteous. So within three years, he had three restaurants operating in Washington, and more would soon follow.

Of course, interesting problems remained, even for so streamlined an operation. For instance, root beer had to be served in frosted mugs, especially in the summer, but the city demanded hot water dishwashing. The result: quite a few of the clean, hot mugs cracked when they were put into the cooler. Since the mugs cost 25 cents apiece, there was ample incentive for a young businessman to develop alternative cleaning procedures. After a long year of arguing, Bill finally convinced Washington to permit cold water, chlorine sterilization.

And on very cold days, the rotisserie produced enough heat so that the nearby plate glass window might crack. But not on October 18, 1928, the day our album begins. That was a day when a tender roast sent out a fragrant invitation, when three working men warmed themselves with hot barbequed pork sandwiches — for fifteen cents each.

II. Dining by headlight— August 4, 1937

Turning the page to our second recollected photograph, the first thing we notice is how large, yet crowded the picture seems. One reason is the darkness of the setting: the moonlight is casting shadows beside each car in the Hot Shoppes parking lot, creating the impression that there are twice as many cars as there really are. A second reason is the hugeness of the

First drive-in—Georgia Ave.

cars — even in relation to the large, rectangular building, with the pitched roof, the automobiles appear to be immense.

The cars are parked at irregular intervals throughout the lot. To the right of the restaurant, a dark sedan sits alone, the driver's profile clearly visible through his open window. The sedan's headlights illuminate the side door of the building, and the young man who has just emerged. From his long stride, it's clear that he's running toward the sedan. The whiteness of his shirt and cap, bathed in the brightness of the headlights, dominates the otherwise dark photo. Alone at the center of this scene, he resembles a Broadway star, singing his final solo to a crowded house.

Meals for Americans on the move
The Thirties

The young man in the white cap actually was on center stage for the Hot Shoppes of the 1930's. It was during this decade that cars came to occupy a central place in America, and drive-in service grew proportionally, with the Hot Shoppes leading the way on the East Coast. Bill Marriott hired hundreds of drive-in waiters, who came to be called "Running Boys" in 1934. Their job was to hurry out to parked cars, take orders, run them to the kitchen, and then return running with the food on trays that they carried over their heads. A tray would then be attached to the side of the car. To inform a Running Boy that service was required, cars flashed their headlights, although the Running

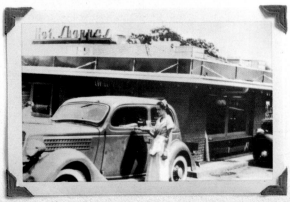

Boys were usually on their way before the drivers got around to doing that. Quite clearly, Hot Shoppes policy required the waiters to be fast— although the restaurants' brief experiment with roller skating waiters was terminated when their added speed was weighed against the increase in broken dishes.

The Running Boy actually

Bill and Alice Marriott's understanding of the role of the automobile in their business extended beyond drive-in service. In accordance with E.M. Statler's formula for success in the hospitality industry—"location, location, location"—they set out to discover which locations around Washington experienced the most traffic. They counted cars, in the morning, the afternoon, and sometimes through

became the logo for the Hot Shoppes, and he was an appropriate symbol. From their inception, the Hot Shoppes were dedicated to serving Americans on the move. In fact, the first Hot Shoppe opened on the very day that the most daring American on the move, Charles Lindbergh, took off on his non-stop solo flight across the Atlantic.

the night. They noted which direction enjoyed the steadier flow, and where cars parked in greater number. Then they rented the properties in the busiest sites, and secured permits to alter curbs to facilitate parking as well as curbside service. And the Hot Shoppes succeeded, and continued to grow in number.

As their clientele expanded, the Marriotts chose to diversify their menu beyond the spicy barbeque and Mexican food. They hired Mrs. Iva Savage, a kitchen and menu consultant from Schrafft's, considered at the time to be the finest restaurant chain in the United States. She added soups, entreés, sandwiches, and an assortment of pastries and breads. She also supervised the operation of a two-story commissary to assist in the preparation of baked goods, and later a selection of American and European soups, salads, and desserts.

Throughout this decade of rapid growth, however, the Hot Shoppes never changed their focus: efficient service, fair prices, and an attention to people on the move. So when people began moving by plane in greater numbers, the Hot Shoppes became the first restaurants to serve meals for the airline passengers. Actually, at first the Fourteenth Street Bridge Hot Shoppes served the passengers and the flight crews at the restaurant itself. But when the customers began ordering their food "to go" with greater frequency, the Marriotts decided it would be easier to simply deliver meals to the planes at Hoover Field, just across the road. Bill's brother Paul supervised the "In-Flite" service, which began in 1937 with simple box lunches, and then developed full meals kept warm in an insulated carrier and delivered to the DC-3's by a custom-designed truck with a loading deck on the roof.

"In-Flight" Catering

As the decade closed, the idea of the Hot Shoppes Running Boy was still thriving; his territory, however, had expanded from the parking lot to the airport runway.

III. A very early supper— December 16, 1943

For an indoor picture, this one has extremely fine detail, probably because the flash attachments developed for press photography improved so greatly in the Thirties and Forties. Whatever the reason, we can clearly discern the expressions on the faces of the diners seated in the square central area. We can even make out the sweet, conspiratorial wink one waitress is giving to another, as the former enters the room from a doorway at the rear.

The room is crowded, every booth and table occupied, most of them filled. From the sunlight streaming through the window, it's obvious that it's about mid-day, although we have no way of sharpening our estimate. Even the food fails to give us a clue: many of the plates have rolls and bowls of what appears to be breakfast cereal, but others have large salads, with fruits, or chicken, or tuna.

Each table has a vase with a fresh flower, a napkin dispenser, salt and pepper shakers, and a small pitcher of milk. Surprisingly, there is no sugar or butter in sight.

The parking lot is visible through the low windows on the right side of the photograph. The lot is empty, even though the restaurant is so full.

Rationing, without tightening belts too much
The Forties

This picture tells us a great deal about America, and particularly Washington, during the war years. Begin with the parking lot. It's empty because citizens were conserving as much fuel as possible, to be shipped overseas in support of the military effort. To discourage the private use of automobiles, the Hot Shoppes suspended curbside service during the war years.

That the restaurant is so crowded reflects both the popularity of Hot Shoppes, as well as the suddenly increased population of the nation's capitol. Many people came to the area to help the war effort, in factories and in administrative services. And because there were so many, in so short a period of time, there was inadequate full-service housing. Quite a few lived in single rooms: to dine, they had to go to restaurants.

By the 1940's, the Hot Shoppes served from early in the morning to well past midnight, so they could accommodate the steady flow to and from offices and homes; as well as from the night-shift at the munitions factories. All of which helps to explain why people at a single table might be eating either breakfast or dinner. In America's busiest city, people were running at full speed around the clock.

The menu also changed with the War. Because of meat rationing, entree

salads, vegetable platters, and souffles were introduced, and quickly gained popularity. The salads we see in the picture are more likely to be made with chicken rather than tuna; although poultry was rationed, there was some available. Virtually all the

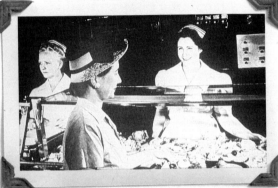

canned fish, however, was sent overseas. Eggs were also claimed by the armed forces, converted to powdered form, and shipped to our soldiers. Butter was not served at all in American restaurants. And since sugar was scarce, it was removed from the regular table setting. Mrs. Savage, however, was able to convert many recipes from sugar to more plentiful substitutes, such as "King Syrup," which resembled today's Karo Syrup.

Quality at the Hot Shoppes remained at a high level, despite the rationing. Bill Marriott saw to that. His unannounced inspections, in the true spirit of a Commanding Officer, were legendary. Kitchens had to be efficient, uniforms spotless. It was a rare employee who didn't recognize the

Marriott car, and what it meant: the white glove treatment, from the boiler room to the attic. Usually the warning call came down from the restaurant's offices upstairs — "here comes the Big Tamale" — and the staff passed the message along. That probably explains why one of the waitresses in our photograph is winking to her co-worker.

Consistent quality was also guaranteed by the extensive collection of Recipe Cards, and the training program that supported them. Each Hot Shoppes Manager attended a weekly cooking class, at which he or she would be required to prepare a dish…without advance warning, and without the Recipe Cards. About every month there were written exams as well.

The Marriotts' contribution to the war effort extended beyond rationing. The Hot Shoppes operated service facilities at a number of the military sites in the area—for instance, the radar, rocket-launcher, and B-29 turrets plant in Maryland, and the Naval Communications Annex at Ward Circle, in Washington. The Hot Shoppe at the Fourteenth Street Bridge, Number Eight, was also especially busy preparing food for the increased number of military airplanes and also serving passengers on the ground. Bob Hope and his USO troupe were a common sight at that Hot Shoppe, enjoying home-style food before taking off to entertain the troops.

The experience gained in such operations served the Marriotts and the country well following the war, after our soldiers had returned from Europe and Asia, and were working energetically to rebuild a peacetime economy. Factories and businesses and shopping centers needed cafeterias, and the Marriotts had learned how to run them. Not that the Hot Shoppes had diminished! To the contrary, they actually had grown during the decade. But they wanted to move into new areas, and more quickly, because America had her foot firmly on the accelerator as she rolled into the fifties.

J. W. Marriott, Jr., behind the wheel

The Upshur Street Commissary was also operating at maximum capacity as the Forties drew to a close. Under the direction of J. Mack Woodward, the Commissary became the second largest purchaser of beef in the entire country…just behind the military, coincidentally. Onion rings were cut in unprecedented numbers by a special machine invented by Hot Shoppes' Gene Spangler. Thousands of muffins were baked fresh daily.

And, to welcome the new decade, coffee went from a nickel to a dime (which so anguished Mr. Marriott that he spent two sleepless nights checking with each of the Hot Shoppes to make certain that none of his customers were upset by this change that inflation had forced upon him).

IV. A table for three-and-a-half— June 27, 1956

Our fourth photo is in dazzling color—Kodacolor—so the light hair of the two youngsters seems almost to illuminate their table near the corner window. Spread out on the table are all the props of family travel: a map, binoculars, the baby boy's rattle and "musical duck," the young girl's doll. There's also a brand new Polaroid camera, much bigger than the ones we're used

to seeing. Plus a pair of dark green clip-on sun glasses—probably for the driver—and the baby's sky-blue sun bonnet.

The mid-day sunlight paints the luncheon dishes in lively colors, too. A plate of fried chicken, another plate heaped high with breaded, fried shrimp and cole slaw, and in front of the little girl a hamburger and onion rings. The baby is heartily relishing his thumb. From the way the family is leaning over their servings, it's fair to conclude that their travels have more than fueled their appetites.

Through the window behind the little girl we see a young couple parked in a

moving into "fast food"

sleek silver convertible, outlined in chrome, facing the restaurant. The man, behind the steering wheel, is speaking into what looks a little bit like a parking meter, except that it has a tray attached to it and a small plastic rectangle rising above and behind it. The pretty young woman on the passenger side has long hair, slightly discomposed and swept over her right shoulder. It's likely that her companion has been driving fast, through the wind.

If impatient Americans in the 1950's couldn't bear to wait for their photos to be developed, and if they were restless to get around quickly in their streamlined cars, then they also were impatient for their meals. Which was ideal for the Hot Shoppes, since they had always specialized in serving people on the move.

The Hot Shoppes take to the highways
The Fifties

J.W. Marriott (at window) drops in

Many of the elements in this picture suggest speed, beginning with the large Polaroid camera resting in the middle of the family's table. Photo developing in just sixty seconds, for a country that was impatient, a country beginning its romance with instant things.

The highways accommodated automobiles that were big and moved quickly, and were designed to look fast: long, tapered lines, flaring into wings. A motorist accustomed to the square compact cars of the seventies and eighties would feel he was headed for Mars if he found himself driving one of these powerful, winged vehicles of the mid-1950's. It's also easy to understand why our convertible passenger's long hair is a bit wild: the speed limit on many of our newly built thruways was 65 miles per hour.

To begin with, curb-side service was made even quicker by adding microphones to the operation. Motorists relayed their orders directly to the kitchen through what was named the "Teletray"; swift as they were, Running Boys could not move to the kitchen faster than the electrons transmitted through the microphone system. Then, of course, the Running Boy served the order, running with tray held high. Sometimes, he would be lucky enough to serve Bill Marriott or one of his assistants on a "Silver Dollar" inspection and win a silver dollar. Further, the Teletray hostess would win a silver dollar if she had

observed the four Hot Shoppes rules for courtesy and efficiency when she had taken the order.

Throughout the 1950's, the Hot Shoppes were serving a great deal of food to go: Hot Shoppes dinners such as "Pappy Parker Fried Chicken," presented in distinctive "Pappy Parker" suitcases, and "Shrimp Boxes" were popular among customers who wanted to enjoy prepared food at home. The "Teen Twist" sandwich and the triple decker "Mighty Mo" hamburger were also attracting loyal fans, especially among the younger set. And it was becoming much easier to find Hot Shoppes on the road—both small roads and large. For instance, the Hot Shoppes moved to the New

York State Thruway in 1955, and shortly thereafter to Delaware. With all the new Hot Shoppes, the Marriotts were able to serve more of those Americans who were traveling greater and greater distances.

In fact, the America of the 1950's was doing a great many things on the road, in addition to dining. In unprecedented numbers, baby boom families loaded up their big, comfortable sedans and station wagons, and visited our national parks and cities and farm country. They hiked down the Grand Canyon, up Mount Washington, and

snapped millions of photos of Mount Rushmore and the Empire State Building. They had maps and binoculars and tour guides to help them find the most scenic spots. And when they needed guidance for the even greater adventure, the adventure of parenting, they had Dr. Spock.

The Marriotts were aware that these traveling Americans needed places to stay overnight, and made the momentous decision to move into yet another facet of hospitality: motels and hotels. They opened their first, the Twin Bridges Motor Hotel, in 1957, on land originally belonging to the estate of George Washington Parke Custis, the grandson of Martha Washington. Since that time, under the direction of Bill Marriott's sons, Bill, Jr. and Richard, Marriott Corporation has opened hundreds of additional hotels and resorts, as well as other dining facilities.

But in the Fifties, such developments were just beginning, and the focus of the Hot Shoppes continued to be the family, and increasingly, children. There were 1.59 children in every family, and the Hot Shoppes were among their favorite places. Children saw animated Hot Shoppes vegetables on T.V., then ordered them in junior portions. At the table, they could work at the mathematics and language puzzles in the new edition of *Table Talk*, a monthly Hot Shoppes entertainment publication. In many ways, the the Hot Shoppes had become an adventure for kids.

V. A holiday feast— November 24, 1960

Our fifth recollected snapshot has been enlarged: it covers almost a full page in our scrapbook.

So even the small objects are distinct, and appear to be even more colorful than they are in real life. In the foreground, a long, low bakery display counter. Cookies are arranged in rows on the lower shelf; on the narrower upper shelf, cakes and pies. Some of the pies are obscured by the natural light reflecting off the protective plate glass. To the right of the counter, a squat freezer display case. Visible through the glass top of the case are long rows of the kind of cylindrical containers usually used for selling pints of ice cream. To the right of the ice cream case, a sales counter with a cash register.

In the background, a tall, glassed-in display case, with many shelves filled with breads, rolls, and more cakes and pies (we can't see the lower shelves, because the pastry counter is blocking them). Along the top of the high display case, large white letters spelling out "Hot Shoppes Pantry House." Above and behind the case we can easily discern the pattern of the wallpaper: hens and roosters.

There are three people in the photograph. A dark-haired woman in a white uniform stands behind the counter, and on the opposite side two women in lightweight car coats. Two large square packages rest on the counter. Their silvery covering catches the sunlight and blurs the picture slightly, although we can read the large cheerful lettering along the side of each box: "Happy Holidays — Hot Shoppes."

The housewife's best friend
The Sixties

Before the microwave revolution, overworked housewives turned to Hot Shoppes' Pantry Houses for home-style cooking on those occasions when they simply didn't have the time to prepare their families' favorites. Or on those special occasions, like Thanksgiving, when the extended family, and friends, brought holiday appetites too great for even the largest home freezers and ovens. That may be what happened to the two women in our picture, since the two packages on the counter are almost certainly holiday turkeys, with dressing and gravy—prepared upon request by the Hot Shoppes.

The Hot Shoppes were also a family friend on other occasions—whenever someone wanted fresh pastries and breads, shipped daily from the Com-

missary, or premium quality ice cream. These were sold at a Pantry House, which was a retail food outlet built-in as part of the Hot Shoppes. The first Pantry House opened in 1947, and offered a small selection of pastries and ice creams. With the advent of freezer technology, however, their line of products expanded to include a full range of first-rate edibles.

VI. A Sunday dinner—July 20, 1969

Our recollected photograph from the late Sixties looks the oldest, even though it's the product of up-to-date camera and film. Certainly, the quality is modern: high resolution, fine detail, and a wide range of subtly differentiated colors. But there is something in the decorous look of the older couple that suggests an earlier time.

The woman has short, wavy gray hair, combed to one side. Her dress is navy blue, with half-sleeves and a white lace collar. The man is wearing a dark blazer, white shirt and a bow tie. The thin streak of late afternoon sun that reaches their table highlights his thinning silver hair.

Their table is set simply: a vase in the middle, with a flower that matches the color of the man's boutonniere. A bowl of soup rests in front of each of the diners. His soup looks creamy—perhaps it's a bisque or a chowder; hers is a clear broth.

The tables near these two people are unoccupied, which is perhaps the way they want it. They appear to be engaged in conversation, since neither is eating at the moment the photograph is being taken.

The background is relatively dark, except for the light escaping through the half-open, swinging door to the kitchen. Our glimpse of the kitchen is intriguing. An aproned chef is working over a skillet, head tilted forward, intent on his task. Above his head a portable television is turned on. Because the T.V. is turned toward the dining area, we can make out the contours of the picture. With a magnifying glass, we're able to recognize one of the most famous tableaus in modern history—the Apollo 11 lunar module settling on the moon's surface. Since the space camera is attached to the module itself, only half of the vehicle can be filmed during landing. But there's no mistaking that scene.

Our diners are smiling at each other, undistracted by the television behind them.

A haven for tradition
The Seventies

Sunday, July 20, 1969 may have been mankind's giant leap to the moon, and into the Seventies, but our two diners have perhaps themselves turned seventy, and take a somewhat broader view of our century. They're less concerned with outer space, more preoccupied with inner satisfaction—the reliable, social habit of a Sunday dinner. In a quiet, sit-down restaurant serving traditional American dishes.

Two details strike us immediately—the man's boutonniere, and the flower on the table. Both are seemingly inconsequential. How much effort, after all, does it take to cut a carnation or a mum, and pin it to a lapel, or place it in a vase? But it is in the holding to such rituals that people and institutions honor occasions: the sense that there is something or someone worth dignifying with special attention.

The fact that both diners have their soup before them is interesting. In the recent past, Americans haven't cooked or ordered soup as frequently as in earlier years. Perhaps a nation committed to winning the race to the moon didn't have the luxury of simmering vegetables, of seasoning to

taste, of waiting for the soup to cool just enough to be savored, and of slowly enjoying, spoon-by-spoon. Bill Marriott, however, was very much committed to the quality of Hot Shoppes soups, especially the Chicken Noodle Soup; for many years, even with his rigorous system of recipe cards, he would permit only the Commissary to prepare this soup, so that absolute consistency could be maintained.

It would be a mistake to suggest that this muted scene indicates that the America of the Seventies is slowing down, or that the Hot Shoppes have shifted their focus. The Hot Shoppes, and the corporation that stand behind them, continued their commitment to serving Americans on the move. Hot Shoppes cafeterias grew in number and size, in Europe as well as

America, and accommodated increasing numbers of diners at work or shopping or socializing. But it's also reassuring to see in this remembered photograph the vitality of American traditions, such as the peaceful Sunday dinner.

VII. Opening the new Hot Shoppes— May 20, 1987

Like the last page of any album, our final reminiscence is the most recent. So recent, indeed, it's almost not accurate to call it a reminiscence— except that it's a newspaper photo, and therefore already has yellowed slightly.

Since our picture is black-and-white, it's hard to judge the time of day, but we can speculate about the weather. The two umbrellas in the center of the scene tell that story.

Beneath the umbrellas we see a woman in a raincoat, escorted toward a building by a man in a formal, dark suit with bright pocket silk. Flanking them and holding the umbrellas are two young women, dressed in white uniforms and caps similar to those of the Running Boys. The "Running Girls" make us wonder if perhaps this scene is much earlier than the date across the top of the newspaper. Our curiosity is reinforced by the cars parked along the curb, in the right foreground. Judging from the square shape of the large passenger compartments, the vehicles date from the Twenties or Thirties.

In the very center of the scene is a large banner, running above the open side of a large, square tent. The banner reads "Grand Opening Hot Shoppes," and to the left of the banner, in smaller letters, a logo with the words "Sixtieth: Marriott."

In the upper right hand corner of the picture, toward the rear of the tent, we can just make out four standing musicians. Their instruments are raised, probably signalling that a party has begun.

A tradition of renewal
The Eighties

Bill and Alice Marriott's idea for the Hot Shoppes has thrived because it has at its heart two enduring principles, which are cogently expressed in these two Hot Shoppes slogans: "food for the entire family," and "square meals at a fair price." Sociability and value. That's why Marriott continues to open new Hot Shoppes, such as the one that is featured in our newspaper photograph.

The event captured in our photo, however, is not just any opening. It is the celebration of the Sixtieth Anniversary of Bill Marriott's first restaurant, the A & W stand on Fourteenth Street. So the Marriott family chose to honor the historic quality of the day by traveling with honored friends to the restaurant in cars that evoke the early days of the Hot Shoppes. Moreover, there is an historic quality to the address of the new Hot Shoppe — 1750 Pennsylvania Avenue, within two blocks of the White House. If it's fair to say that the Hot Shoppes have reflected the changing quality of American life, it's also fair to say that the Hot Shoppes have been close to the center of American life.

The cars, however, aren't the only traditional element in the event portrayed. The two "Running Girls" in their bright starched uniforms are emblems of Bill Marriott's dedication to friendly service in clean facilities. They are the fruition of his close supervision, and his close friendships with so many valued co-workers.

Once inside this brand new Hot Shoppes, customers will also witness Hot Shoppes' continuing effort to serve working Americans: a catering service for offices in the vicinity.

The recipes assembled in the *Marriott Hot Shoppes Cookbook* are also offered in the spirit of continuity and innovation. They represent the enduring styles of American cookery, which also means that they embrace many different regions and the influence of many nationalities. And they reflect tastes that have evolved over the years. Remember, the first Hot Shoppe served a short menu of barbeque sandwiches, tamales, and chili con carne; the new Pennsylvania Avenue Hot Shoppe offers a full selection of soups, salads, quiches, sandwiches, entrees, and pastries.

It's a menu that has retained popular items, and added new dishes that will interest people in all age groups, and from all walks of life: it's the tradition of sixty years of American cookery.

The new look

THE HOT SHOPPES RECIPES

Collating and adapting the Hot Shoppes recipes has been a challenging and elaborate task, but we feel we've succeeded in writing instructions that will enable you to create at home the textures, aromas, and flavors you associate with your favorite Hot Shoppes meals. If you've never eaten at any of the Hot Shoppes, these recipes will certainly introduce you to the best of our sixty years of culinary experimentation and success.

Experimentation is an issue that merits further discussion. In order to come as close as possible to Hot Shoppes tastes, you should resist the temptation to experiment. Follow the recipes closely—for instance, where we recommend using McCormick spices. Whenever we make such a recommendation, it's because that product is precisely what we use in the Hot Shoppes.

You will not be able to use the brands we use in every case, however, because some of our ingredients are available only to restaurants. In those instances, we have invariably adapted the recipes to similar ingredients that can easily be found in your own neighborhood grocery store or supermarket.

One additional reason for the authenticity of these recipes is that we have derived them from Mr. Marriott's original Recipe Cards and Emergency Recipe Cards. These were developed by our chief chefs and commissary supervisors down through the years to create uniformity in our kitchens. The Recipe Cards were for everyday use, and the Emergency Cards were for those situations when an ingredient was unavailable, or when items normally supplied from our central commissary were delayed. Of course, all of these recipe cards call for much greater amounts of ingredients, so we at Marriott Corporation have tailored them for family use, trimming them for servings of 6–8.

Naturally, many of you will also seek to further tailor the recipes to your own preference. The barbeque sauces, for instance, might tempt you to new heights of peppery zest…which would be in keeping with Bill Marriott's original plan for the Hot Shoppes: hearty meals that would shield against the sting of winter.

But whether you follow these recipes to the letter, or use them as more general inspiration, you'll be able to recreate and enjoy these enduring American dishes.

A&W Root Beer in Frosted Mug

BEVERAGES

We begin with beverages because the Hot Shoppes actually began as A & W Root Beer stands, the first one opening on May 20, 1927.

If our recipe for A & W Root Beer in a Frosty Mug seems especially detailed, remember that the Marriotts' A & W stands suffered through quite a few heat-cracked mugs in the early days. We're trying to spare you that expense. We're also trying to spare you a messy overflow when, for the A & W Root Beer float, we advise you to place the scoop of ice cream in the glass before you pour in the root beer. Trust us.

The other variable to keep in mind when making these refreshing drinks is mixing time. If, for instance, you blend the Orange Freeze for too long, the sherbet separates, and a watery consistency results. The remedy is to add more sherbet, and blend again—briefly.

It is not quite so easy to over-mix the Thick Shakes, although that too can happen. In any case, after years of serving thick shakes to millions of Americans, we've learned that no two like theirs the same way. Some prefer them so thick a straw will stand up straight—so you may wish to exceed our recommendations on the amount of ice cream for this recipe.

A & W ROOT BEER IN FROSTED MUG

A & W Root Beer, cold   *As Needed*

PREPARATION:
1. All A & W Root Beer *must* be served in frozen mugs and never with ice.
✱2. Freeze mugs by placing *clean, dry, room temperature* mugs in freezer.
3. Remove frozen mugs from freezer as needed, taking care not to bang mugs together.
4. Fill each mug to within one inch from rim by tilting mug on an angle as the root beer is poured down the side of the mug.
✱5. Serve with a straw.

Note: Do not place hot mugs in freezer, as mugs will break.

A & W ROOT BEER FLOAT

A & W Root Beer, cold   1¼ cups (approx.)
Vanilla Ice Cream   1 scoop (approx. 2⅔ tbsp.)

YIELD: 1 serving

PREPARATION:
* 1. Freeze 14 – 16 ounce soda glasses by placing *clean, dry, room temperature* glasses in freezer.
2. Remove glasses from freezer as needed.
3. Place 1 scoop of vanilla ice cream in bottom of frosted soda glass.
4. Fill soda glass with root beer to within 1 inch of the rim of the glass, tilting glass on an angle as the root beer is poured down the side of the glass.
5. Serve with a straw and a soda spoon.

*NOTE:
– Do not place hot glasses in freezer, as glasses will break.

LEMONADE WITH SHERBET

Lemonade—fresh or reconstituted from frozen	*As Needed*
*Lemon Sherbet	*1 scoop (approx. 2⅔ tbsp.)*
Lemon Slice, ¼" thick	*1 each*
Maraschino Cherry, half	*1 each*
Fresh Mint	*1 sprig*
YIELD:	*1 serving*

PREPARATION:
1. Place lemonade in glass to within 2 inches of top of glass and fill glass to within 1½ inches of the top of the glass with ice.
2. Add 1 scoop of lemon sherbet.
3. Garnish with slice of lemon on the side of the glass.
4. Place ½ maraschino cherry and a sprig of fresh mint on top of the sherbet.
5. Serve with a straw and a soda spoon.

*NOTE:
— If desired, orange sherbet may be used instead of lemon sherbet.

ORANGE FREEZE

Orange Juice—fresh or reconstituted from frozen	*¾ cup*
Orange Sherbet	*1 cup*
Orange Slice, twisted—¼" thick or Maraschino Cherry, quarter	*1 each*
Fresh Mint	*1 sprig*
YIELD:	*1 serving*

PREPARATION:
* 1. Freeze 14—16 ounce soda glasses by placing *clean, dry, room temperature* glasses in freezer.
2. Remove glasses from freezer as needed.
3. Place orange juice and orange sherbet in a blender and mix until well-blended (to the consistency of a milkshake).
4. Pour orange freeze mixture into frosted soda glass to within ½ inch from the top of the glass.
5. Garnish top with a whole orange slice twisted or ¼ maraschino cherry and a sprig of fresh mint.
6. Serve with a straw and a soda spoon.

*NOTE:
— Do not place hot glasses in freezer, as glasses will break. — If overblended, mixture may become thin and watery. If this occurs, add additional sherbet, one scoop at a time, until the desired consistency is reached.

MILK SHAKE
(Chocolate, Vanilla, Strawberry, Pineapple or Coffee)

*Vanilla Ice Cream	3 scoops (approx. 2⅔ tbsp. each)
Milk	1 cup
Syrup or Topping	⅓ cup
YIELD:	1 Serving

PREPARATION:
1. Place all ingredients in blender container and process on low speed, about 20 to 30 seconds until ingredients are blended thoroughly.
2. Pour into a frosted goblet or large soda glass.
3. Serve with a straw and a soda spoon.

*NOTE:
— Use Strawberry Ice Cream for the Strawberry Milk Shake and Coffee Ice Cream for the Coffee Milk Shake.
— If a stronger flavor of chocolate is desired, Chocolate Ice Cream may be used for the Chocolate Milk Shake.

The thickness of the milk shake may be adjusted by adding or reducing the amount of ice cream added to the shake.

BASIC FRUIT PUNCH

Lemon Juice	½ cup
Orange Juice Concentrate (not diluted)	1¼ cups
Instant Tea	¼ cup
Cold Water	1½ quarts
Sugar	1 cup
Pineapple Juice	1¾ cups
Grapefruit Juice	3 cups
Grape Juice	1 quart
Red Food Coloring, optional	¼ teaspoon
YIELD:	1 gallon

PREPARATION:
1. To use fresh lemons for juice — soften lemons by rolling, then cut in half and squeeze.
2. Measure defrosted orange juice concentrate. Do not dilute.
3. Dissolve instant tea in cold water.
4. Combine all ingredients. Stir well to blend.
5. Chill in refrigerator until time of service.
6. Add approximately 1 quart of crushed ice just before serving.

GARNISH:
1. If desired, garnish with thin slices of oranges which have been cut in quarters. Allow one orange per gallon to garnish.
2. Fresh limes, lemons or strawberries may also be used for garnish.

CRANBERRY PUNCH

Cranberry Juice	*3 cups*
Pineapple Juice	*3 cups*
Ginger Ale	*2 cups*
YIELD:	*2 quarts*

PREPARATION:
1. Blend fruit juices. Chill in refrigerator until ready to serve.
2. Add Ginger Ale and approximately 2 cups of crushed ice just before serving.

Chicken Noodle Soup and Seafood Cocktail

APPETIZERS, SOUPS

There is no fast way to make soup. For example, our Navy Bean Soup requires that you soak the beans overnight, and the instructions alone for our French Onion Soup Au Gratin take about ten minutes to read. So be prepared to spend some time creating these dishes.

But the effort is well worth it, because people also take their time enjoying these soups. They linger over them. For Bill Marriott, the Chicken Noodle Soup was a particular favorite, especially at Sunday dinner. He liked the fact that it was creamier than a clear chicken broth: it seemed to him a more substantial beginning for a meal. Today, this soup is a regular offering at all Hot Shoppes; many, in fact, list it as the "House Soup."

Having suggested that most of these soups require a good deal of time to create, we should also point out that some phases of preparation require very little time, and precise timing. For instance, the Clam Chowder and Oyster Bisque demand that you carefully supervise the cooking of the shellfish. Too long, and the oysters or clams get tough and lose their sweetness.

Most of the appetizers Hot Shoppes have served over the years share two qualities—they're simple, and they're chilled. Our philosophy has been to offer appetizers as a clear alternative to soup: steaming soup for brisk days, cool, tender shrimp cocktails for steamy days.

FRUIT CUP WITH SHERBET

Grapefruit Sections, drained	*1⅓ cups (approx. 1 large, fresh grapefruit)*
Orange Sections, drained	*1 cup (approx. 1 large, fresh orange)*
Pear Halves, canned	*1 cup*
Peach Halves, canned	*1 cup*
Pineapple Tidbits, canned	*1 cup*
Red Delicious Apple	*1 each*
Orange Juice – reconstituted from frozen	*½ cup*
Sherbet, Lemon or Lime	*6 to 8 scoops*
(approx. 2⅔ tablespoons per scoop)	

YIELD: *6 to 8 servings*

PREPARATION:
1. If fresh oranges and grapefruits are used, peel and section.
2. Drain all juice from grapefruit and orange sections.
3. Drain peach and pear halves and pineapple tidbits; dice peaches and pears into ½ " pieces.
4. Add orange juice to fruit sections, diced fruit and pineapple tidbits.
5. Wash apple and dice into ½ " cubes. Add to fruit and orange juice mixture.
6. Divide fruit mixture with juice evenly among six small dessert dishes.
7. Garnish each serving with one scoop of sherbet.

NOTE:
— If canned grapefruit and orange sections are used, drain thoroughly.
  DO NOT USE THIS JUICE.
— For an alternate garnish, top each serving with 3 slices of banana (dipped in orange or lemon juice to prevent darkening), a fresh mint sprig and ½ of a maraschino cherry *or* 3 slices of fresh strawberry and a mint sprig.

SEAFOOD COCKTAIL

Perch or Flounder—fresh or thawed from frozen	*1 pound*
Cold Water	*½ cup*
Oleo Margarine	*2 tablespoons*
Salt	*Dash*
White Pepper	*Dash*
Fresh or Frozen Shrimp—peeled and deveined, broken pieces	*1⅔ cups (12 ounces)*
Cold Water	*1 cup*
Salt	*Dash*
Bay Leaf	*1 each*
Peppercorns	*2 each*
Lettuce Leaves	*12 each*
Lettuce, shredded	*2 cups*
Fresh Parsley	*6 sprigs*
Lemon Wedge, ⅛th cut	*6 each*
Saltine Crackers	*24 each*
Cocktail Sauce	*1 cup*
YIELD:	*6 servings*

PREPARATION:

— To Cook Fish Fillets
1. Preheat oven to 325°F.
2. Wash fish fillets and place in a 2-quart baking pan.
3. Dissolve salt and pepper in ½ cup of cold water and pour over fish.
4. Cut oleo margarine into small pieces and place on top of fish.
5. Cover baking pan with aluminum foil and bake in a preheated 325°F oven for 12–15 minutes until fish is tender. Fish is cooked when its color changes *from* clear *to* milky off-white in color. DO NOT OVERCOOK.
6. If fillets have skin on, remove skin from fish. Break fish into ¾" flakes, not chunks or shreds.
7. Hold flaked fish in a pan covered with aluminum foil or plastic film and refrigerate until time of use.

— To Cook Shrimp Pieces
1. Combine water and salt. Bring to a boil.
2. Add bay leaf and peppercorns to boiling water.
3. Add frozen shrimp pieces.
4. Allow water to return to a boil and cook *for only 2 minutes* or until shrimp turn pink. DO NOT OVERCOOK.
5. Drain immediately. Discard seasonings.
6. Place shrimp in a shallow stainless steel pan; cover with ice, refrigerate and allow to chill rapidly.

7. Remove shrimp from ice when chilled. Do not allow shrimp to soak in ice water.
8. Remove any dark spots or shells before using as directed for Seafood Cocktail.
9. Combine chilled flaked fish with the chilled shrimp and store covered under refrigeration until time of use.

— To Assemble Cocktail
1. Place 2 each lettuce leaves on each of 6 individual small salad plates or bowls to line.
2. Place ⅓ cup of shredded lettuce on top of each lettuce-lined plate/bowl.
3. Place ¾ cup of fish and shrimp mixture on top of shredded lettuce.
4. Top each fish/shrimp portion with 1½ tablespoons of cocktail sauce and one each lemon wedge as desired.
5. Garnish each plate with 1 each parsley sprig placed to the side of the fish.

COOKING PEELED AND DEVEINED SHRIMP
FOR APPETIZERS, SALADS OR SALAD MIXTURES

Fresh or Frozen Shrimp—peeled and deveined; whole or broken	*3 pounds*
Salt	*2½ teaspoons*
Cold Water	*8 cups*
Bay Leaf	*3 each*
Peppercorns	*8 each*

YIELD: *Cooked weight of shrimp = 2 pounds 8 ounces*

PREPARATION:
1. Combine water and salt. Bring to a boil.
2. Place bay leaves and 8 peppercorns in a double cheesecloth. Tie cloth and drop in boiling water.
3. Add 3 pounds of fresh or frozen peeled and deveined shrimp to boiling water.
4. Allow water to return to a boil and cook *for only 2 minutes* or until shrimp turns pink. Do not overcook.
5. Drain immediately. Discard seasonings in cheesecloth.
6. Place shrimp in a shallow stainless steel pan; cover with ice, refrigerate and allow to chill rapidly.
7. Remove shrimp from ice when chilled. Do not allow shrimp to soak in ice water.
8. Store shrimp covered under refrigeration until time of use.
9. Remove any dark spots or shells before using in appetizers, salads or salad mixtures.

*NOTE: If using frozen shrimp, do not thaw. Cook from frozen state.

SHRIMP COCKTAIL

Whole Shrimp, cooked—peeled and deveined	*6 each*
Lettuce Leaves	*2 each*
Lettuce, shredded	*⅓ cup*
Fresh Parsley	*1 sprig*
Lemon Wedge, ⅛th cut	*1 each*
Saltine Crackers	*4 each*
Cocktail Sauce	*1½ tablespoons*
YIELD:	*1 serving*

PREPARATION:
1. Place lettuce leaves on individual small salad plate or bowl to line.
2. Place shredded lettuce on top of lettuce leaves.
3. Arrange chilled shrimp on top of the shredded lettuce.
4. Garnish with parsley sprig and place the lemon wedge at the side of the plate/bowl next to the parsley with rind facing upward.
5. Serve with saltine crackers and cocktail sauce.

CLAM DIP

Cream Cheese	*8 oz. (1 cup)*
Worcestershire Sauce	*2½ teaspoons*
Tartar Sauce	*½ cup*
Onion, finely grated	*1 tablespoon*
Salt	*To Taste*
White Pepper	*½ teaspoon*
Clams, drained—finely chopped	*½ cup*
YIELD:	*Approximately 2 cups*

PREPARATION:
1. Hold cream cheese at room temperature until soft enough to cream.
2. Beat until creamy and smooth.
3. Add Worcestershire sauce, tartar sauce, salt, pepper and grated onion to cream cheese. Continue beating to blend thoroughly.
4. Add drained, finely chopped clams and blend into the cheese mixture.
5. Cover and refrigerate until time of service.
6. Serve as a "dip" with fresh vegetables, potato chips or specialty crackers as desired.

CELERY STUFFED WITH HERB,
SPRING OR PIMIENTO COTTAGE CHEESE

Celery Stalks	*As Needed: 3 to 3½" length*
Herb Cottage Cheese	
Spring Onion (with tops), finely chopped	*⅔ cup*
Tender Celery Leaves, finely chopped	*2 tablespoons*
Salt	*¼ teaspoon*
White Pepper	*Dash*
Cottage Cheese	*1 pound*
Spring Cottage Cheese	
Carrots, ⅛" dice	*1 tablespoon*
Radishes, ⅛" dice	*1½ teaspoons*
Chives or Spring Onions, finely chopped	*1½ teaspoons*
Cottage Cheese	*1 pound*
Salt	*1 teaspoon*
White Pepper	*¼ teaspoon*
Pimiento Cheese	
Cottage Cheese	*1 pound*
Salt	*¼ teaspoon*
Pimiento, ⅛" dice	*¼ cup*
YIELD:	*6 to 8 individual servings*
	20 buffet servings

PREPARATION: – (Prepare Cheese Variety Desired)

Herb Cottage Cheese
1. Chop the onions with the tops and the celery leaves very fine.
2. Add the salt and the pepper to chopped herbs and combine with cheese. Mix well to blend.

Spring Cottage Cheese
3. Peel carrots and shred or chop finely into ⅛" pieces.
4. Cut ends from radishes. Wash radishes and shred or chop finely into ⅛" pieces.
5. Combine carrots, radishes, chives, salt and pepper with cottage cheese. Mix well to blend.

Pimiento Cheese
6. Add salt and diced pimiento to cottage cheese.
7. Mix *just* enough to blend.
8. Clean the celery stalks and if small ones are used, leave on a little of the white leaves.

9. Stuff the celery with Herb, Spring or Pimiento Cottage Cheese as desired.
10. Cover and refrigerate until time of service.

NOTE:
— For individual servings, line each dish with a crisp lettuce leaf. Fill each stalk with cheese. Place 3 stuffed stalks on lettuce.
— If desired, garnish with parsley or watercress sprig, pimiento strips, carrot curl, or green pepper ring.

DEVILED OR STUFFED EGGS

Eggs, raw — uncooked	*6 each*
Salt	*To Taste*
White Pepper	*To Taste*
Dill Pickle, finely chopped	*1½ tablespoons*
Mustard, prepared	*½ teaspoon*
Mayonnaise	*¼ cup*
YIELD:	*12 Deviled Egg Halves*

PREPARATION:
1. Place eggs in saucepan and cover with cold water (at least 1 inch above eggs).
2. Bring water quickly to a boil; at once, reduce heat to keep water just below simmering.
3. Cook eggs 15 to 20 minutes.
4. Cool at once in cold water — this helps prevent a dark surface from forming on the yolks and allows for easier peeling.
5. When eggs have cooled, cut eggs in half lengthwise.
6. Remove yolks and press through a sieve or mash with a fork.
7. In a separate bowl, combine mayonnaise, mustard, salt, white pepper and stir to blend well.
8. Combine finely chopped dill pickle with seasoned mayonnaise and blend with the cooked egg yolks.
9. Refill egg whites with yolk mixture using a fork or a pastry bag with a large enough tip to allow finely chopped pickle to go through.
10. If desired, garnish the top of each deviled egg half with a thinly sliced olive.

CHOPPED CHICKEN LIVERS

Milk	*½ cup*
Salt	*2 teaspoons*
Chicken Livers	*1¾ cups*
Rendered Chicken Fat	*¾ cup*
Onions, finely chopped	*1 cup*
White Pepper	*¼ teaspoon*
YIELD:	*6 to 8 servings*

TO RENDER CHICKEN FAT
- Place chicken fat in a heavy sauce pan over low heat.
- Simmer slowly until pieces of fat are crisp and all water is evaporated. The color should be golden yellow.
- Strain. Excess may be frozen. Use as directed.

PREPARATION:
1. Thaw chicken livers. Remove all fat or fiber between liver sections.
2. Mix salt with milk. Soak livers in the salt and milk for at least ½ hour. Wash off milk and drain well.
3. Sauté livers and onions slowly in heated chicken fat. Do not overcook.
4. Add white pepper.
5. Place livers and onions (include all the fat) in a medium-size mixing bowl while still hot and beat until lumps are removed and a smooth paste forms. Add all drained fat to paste.
6. Cover and refrigerate until time of service.
7. For each portion: serve approximately 2 ½ – 3 tablespoons of chopped chicken livers placed in a crisp lettuce cup at one end of a salad platter.
8. Top chicken livers with 2 each thinly sliced onion rings and garnish with fresh parsley.
9. Place 3 sweet pickle sticks on lettuce next to liver.
10. Place 3 slices of snack pumpernickel bread overlapping on other end of platter.

NOTE:
- One cup of raw chicken fat yields approximately ¾ cup of rendered fat.
- If platters are prepared in advance, cover tightly with plastic wrap to prevent pumpernickel from drying out.
- For buffet service, the entire batch of Chopped Chicken Livers may be mounded on a large serving plate or tray. Garnish with parsley, thinly sliced onions and sweet pickle sticks or as desired and serve with snack pumpernickel bread or specialty crackers.

CHICKEN NOODLE SOUP

Chicken Broth	*5 cups*
Oleo Margarine	*5 tablespoons*
All-Purpose Flour	*⅓ cup*
Noodle — Rings, ¼" diameter	*⅔ cup*
Chicken, cooked and diced ¼"	*⅔ cup*
YIELD:	*6 to 8 servings*

PREPARATION:
1. Heat 4 cups of chicken broth to boiling in a two quart sauce pan.
2. Melt oleo margarine in a small sauce pan over low heat. Add flour, stirring well to blend. Do not allow to brown.
3. Add the flour and oleo mixture to the boiling stock and cook until thickened over moderate heat.
4. Bring remaining *1* cup of chicken broth to boiling in a small sauce pan. Add the noodles; cook *just* until tender, but not soft.
5. Add the undrained cooked noodles and the cooked diced chicken to the first thickened broth.
6. Taste to adjust seasoning levels.
7. If not served immediately, hold over low heat in a double boiler until time of service.

NOTE:
— Should noodle rings not be available at your local grocery, the following products are recommended as alternatives, miniature bow ties or star noodles (Stelline 59), Ditalini 36, or Tubettini 39.
— If larger noodles are used, they should be cooked according to package directions and drained prior to adding to the thickened broth.
— Depending on the brand of chicken broth used, finished color may range from pale to deep yellow.

CLEAR VEGETABLE SOUP

Beef Broth	*5 ½ cups*
Tomatoes, canned—with juice ¼"–½" dice	*1 ½ cups*
Celery, ¼"–½" dice	*½ cup*
Cabbage, ¼"–½" dice	*⅔ cup*
Green Beans, 1" length	*¼ cup*
Baby Lima Beans	*⅓ cup*
Onions, ¼"–½" dice	*¾ cup*
Carrots, ¼"–½" dice	*½ cup*
Potatoes, ¼"–½" dice	*¾ cup*
Peas	*⅓ cup*
Corn	*⅓ cup*
White Pepper	*To Taste*

YIELD: *6 to 8 servings*

PREPARATION:
1. Add celery, cabbage, green beans, onions, carrots and potatoes to beef broth. Cover and simmer for 30–45 minutes or until vegetables are tender.
2. Add remaining vegetables, including tomatoes with juice and simmer an additional 15 minutes.

Note: Taste soup for seasoning and adjust as desired.

OLD FASHIONED VEGETABLE SOUP

Beef Stock	*6 cups*
Carrots, ¼"–½" dice	*⅔ cup*
Celery, ¼"–½" dice	*⅔ cup*
Potatoes, ¼"–½" dice	*½ cup*
Onion, ¼"–½" dice	*⅔ cup*
Lima Beans	*⅓ cup*
Corn	*⅓ cup*
Peas	*⅓ cup*
Tomatoes, canned — with juice, ¼"–½" dice	*1½ cups*
White Pepper	*⅛ teaspoon*
Flour, all purpose	*3 tablespoons*
Cold Water	*½ cup*

YIELD: *6 to 8 servings*

PREPARATION:
1. Dice vegetables into ¼"–½" pieces and add vegetables (except tomatoes) to the beef stock. Add white pepper.
2. Cover and simmer for 30–45 minutes or until vegetables are tender.
3. Add remaining vegetables, including tomatoes with juice, and simmer an additional 15 minutes.
4. Add flour to the *cold* water and mix well with a wire whip until all lumps are dissolved.
5. Add the flour mixture to the soup, stirring constantly until completely blended and soup has thickened.
6. Taste soup for seasoning and adjust as desired.

SPLIT PEA SOUP

*Ham, finely diced	⅔ cup
Green Split Peas, dried	2¼ cups
Water	2 quarts
Salt Pork, ¼" dice	⅓ cup
Celery, ½" dice	¼ cup
Onions, ½" dice	⅔ cup
Oleo Margarine	3 tablespoons
Flour, all purpose	2 tablespoons
Salt	To Taste
White Pepper	¼ teaspoon
YIELD:	6 to 8 servings

PREPARATION:
1. Wash split peas and allow to soak overnight in 1 quart + 1 cup of water. (Or, simmer gently for 2 minutes, then soak 1 hour.)
2. Cook in the same water. Add diced onion and celery; bring to a boil.
3. Cover, reduce heat and simmer approximately 1½ hours or until peas become soft and begin to break apart. Strain peas through a wire mesh strainer.
4. Dice salt pork into ¼" pieces. Braise salt pork and diced ham. Add remaining 3 cups of water and strained peas.
6. In a small skillet or sauté pan, melt oleo margarine and add flour, stirring to blend well.
7. When oleo margarine and flour mixture begins to bubble, remove from heat and add to strained pea mixture, stirring constantly while blending and until mixture thickens.
8. Add salt and white pepper. Taste soup for seasoning and adjust as desired.

*NOTE:
— If a stronger ham flavor is desired, a meaty ham bone can be cooked with the split peas in Preparation Step #3. At the end of the 1½ hour cooking period, remove ham bone from soup and allow to cool slightly. Cut off meat and dice. Return meat to soup and proceed with Preparation Step #4.

CHICKEN SOUP WITH RICE

Water	*5 cups*
Chicken Base	*2 tablespoons*
Chicken Broth	*3 cups*
Onion, ¼"–½" dice	*1 cup*
Celery, ¼"–½" dice	*1 cup*
Rice, Medium or Long Grain	*1 cup*
White Pepper	*To Taste*
Chicken, cooked – ¼"–½" dice	*1 cup*
YIELD:	*6 to 8 servings*

PREPARATION:
1. Add water to chicken base. Stir to blend thoroughly.
2. Combine diluted chicken base with chicken broth.
3. Add diced onion, celery, rice and white pepper to broth.
4. Bring to a boil; reduce heat and simmer approximately 15–20 minutes or until rice is tender.
5. Add diced chicken to soup and allow to cook an additional 5 minutes or until chicken is heated thoroughly.
6. Taste soup for seasoning and adjust as desired.

NAVY BEAN SOUP

Navy Beans, dry	1 cup
Water	1 quart
Onion, ¼" dice	⅓ cup
Celery, ¼" dice	¼ cup
Carrots, ¼" dice	⅓ cup
Garlic, minced	To Taste
Salt	To Taste
White Pepper	To Taste
Ham Stock	4⅔ cups
Salt Pork, ¼" dice	2 tablespoons
*Ham, finely diced	⅔ cup
Tomato Puree	½ cup
Oleo Margarine	3 tablespoons
Flour, all purpose	2 tablespoons

YIELD: 6 to 8 servings

PREPARATION:
1. Thoroughly wash and pick over beans. Drain.
2. Cover with water and allow to soak overnight. (Or, simmer gently for 2 minutes then soak 1 hour.) Cook in the same water.
3. Dice salt pork into ¼" pieces and sauté to a light brown. Add minced garlic and continue cooking for approximately 2 minutes.
4. Add onion, celery and carrots to pork and sauté lightly.
5. Mix sautéed vegetables and salt pork with soaked beans, water, tomato puree, salt, white pepper, ham and ham stock.
6. Cover and simmer for approximately 2½–3 hours or until beans are tender.
7. In a small skillet or sauté pan, melt oleo margarine and add flour, stirring to blend well.
8. When oleo margarine and flour mixture begins to bubble, remove from heat and add to the simmering soup mixture, stirring constantly while blending and until mixture thickens.
9. Taste soup for seasoning and adjust as desired.
10. If soup is not served immediately, hold soup *hot,* covered on a double-boiler set-up.

*NOTE:
— If a stronger ham flavor is desired, a meaty ham bone can be cooked with the navy beans in Preparation Step #6. At the end of the 2½–3 hour cooking period, remove ham bone from soup and allow to cool slightly. Cut off the meat and dice. Return meat to soup and proceed with Preparation Step #7.

FRENCH ONION SOUP AU GRATIN

Onions, large (approximately 4-6 each)	*5½ cups*
Oleo Margarine	*2 tablespoons*
Paprika	*¼ teaspoon*
Beef Broth	*6 cups*
Beef Consomme	*2½ cups*
White Pepper	*Dash*
Salt	*To Taste*

CROUTON:
Sandwich Bread	*8 slices*
Oleo Margarine, melted	*4 tablespoons*

CHEESE TOPPING:
Swiss Cheese, grated	*2 cups*
Parmesan Cheese, grated	*½ cup*

YIELD: *8 servings*

PREPARATION:
1. Peel onions. Trim to remove any bruised or discolored areas.
2. Slice onions into ⅛" thick crosswise slices. Cut across slices in two directions, cutting each slice into quarters.

French onion soup au gratin

3. Sauté onions in oleo margarine until lightly browned. Stir frequently to prevent overcooking.
4. Add paprika and stir well to blend thoroughly.
5. Add broth and consomme; simmer slowly for ½ hour.
6. Add white pepper and salt.

CROUTON:
7. Preheat oven to 325°F.
8. Trim crusts from bread.
9. Melt oleo margarine in a small saucepan or skillet.
10. Dip one side of bread in melted oleo margarine.
11. Place each slice of bread "buttered side up" on a greased cookie sheet.
12. Bake in a preheated 325°F oven until golden brown.
13. Remove from oven and allow to cool.
14. Hold, covered, at room temperature until needed for assembly of Onion Soup.

CHEESE MIXTURE:
15. Mix grated Swiss and Parmesan cheeses.
16. Hold, refrigerated, until needed for assembly of Onion Soup.
17. Use approximately ¼ cup of combined cheese mixture as directed for each serving of Onion Soup.

ASSEMBLY AND SERVICE:
18. Place heated Onion Soup in *oven-proof* crocks or bowls.
19. Place one toasted crouton on top of each soup portion.
20. Sprinkle each crouton with combined cheese mixture.
21. *Carefully* place soup crocks on an oven-proof tray or pan and place under a preheated broiler for approximately 45 seconds or until cheese is melted and lightly browned.
22. To serve, place soup crock on a plate to underline and serve with a bouillon or soup spoon.

NOTE:
— Soup is best when prepared one day ahead to allow flavors to mellow. Hold soup covered, under refrigeration. Heat prior to service and proceed with preparation Step 7.
— If round croutons are desired, cut each slice of bread with a large round biscuit cutter prior to toasting.

NEW ENGLAND CLAM CHOWDER

Oleo Margarine or Butter	*9 tablespoons*
Onions, ¼" dice	*1½ cups*
Celery, ¼" dice	*1 cup*
Potatoes, ½" dice	*2 cups*
Clams, canned—with juice, ¼" dice	*2½ cups*
White Pepper	*To Taste*
Thyme	*To Taste*
Tabasco Sauce	*¼ teaspoon*
Salt	*2 teaspoons*
Milk	*5 cups*
Flour, all purpose	*½ cup*
Half and Half	*⅓ cup*
YIELD:	*6 to 8 servings*

PREPARATION:
1. Melt 7 tablespoons of oleo margarine in a large saucepan over low heat.
2. Blend in flour and allow to cook approximately 2 minutes, stirring often.
3. Gradually add 5 cups of milk to the flour and oleo margarine mixture. Heat slowly, stirring constantly until mixture thickens and bubbles.
4. Melt the remaining 2 tablespoons of oleo margarine in a small saucepan.
5. Add the diced raw onions, celery and potatoes. Cover and cook slowly, stirring frequently, for approximately 8-10 minutes or until potatoes are tender.
6. Add the clams with juice, white pepper, thyme, tabasco and salt. Heat slowly until thoroughly heated.
7. Stir in half and half.
8. If soup is not served immediately, hold soup *hot,* covered on a double-boiler set-up.

NOTE:
— Vegetables may be sautéed with ⅓ cup of diced salt pork, rather than oleo margarine or butter if desired.

Do not boil after clams and half and half are added.

MANHATTAN CLAM CHOWDER

Salt Pork, ¼" dice	⅓ cup
Onion, ¼" dice	1¾ cups
Celery, ¼" dice	1¼ cups
Green pepper, ¼" dice	¼ cup
Potatoes, ¼" dice	1¾ cups
Tomatoes, canned and drained (reserving juice) ¼" dice	1 cup
Tomato Juice, reserved plus water	1 quart
Tomato Puree	3 tablespoons
Thyme	To Taste
Paprika	¼ teaspoon
Salt	1½ teaspoons
White Pepper	¼ teaspoon
Clams, canned with juice	1½ cups
Oleo Margarine	6 tablespoons
Flour, all purpose	½ cup
Worcestershire Sauce	1 teaspoon
YIELD:	6 to 8 servings

PREPARATION:

1. Dice pork into ¼" pieces and sauté.
2. Dice vegetables into ¼" pieces and add to sautéed pork.
3. Cook slowly about 10 minutes until vegetables are tender, not brown.
4. Drain juice from clams and reserve. If clams are large, dice into ¼" pieces.
5. Combine salt pork and sautéed vegetables with clams, clam juice, tomato juice, water, thyme, paprika, salt, white pepper, diced tomatoes, Worcestershire sauce, and tomato puree.
6. Cover and simmer for approximately 10 minutes.
7. In a small skillet or sauté pan, melt oleo margarine and add flour, stirring to blend well.
8. When oleo margarine and flour mixture begins to bubble, remove from heat and add to simmering soup mixture, stirring constantly while blending and until the mixture thickens, approximately 5 minutes.
9. Taste soup for seasoning and adjust as desired.

NOTE: If soup is not served immediately, hold soup _hot_, covered on a double-boiler set-up.

OYSTER BISQUE

Oleo Margarine or Butter	*8 tablespoons*
Flour, all purpose	*½ cup*
Milk	*5½ cups*
Celery, ¼" dice	*½ cup*
Onions, ¼" dice	*⅓ cup*
Oysters, fresh or canned — with juice, ½" dice	*2 cups*
Salt	*To Taste*
White Pepper	*To Taste*
Cream or Half and Half	*⅓ cup*

YIELD: 6 to 8 servings

PREPARATION:
1. Melt 7 tablespoons of oleo margarine in a large saucepan over low heat.
2. Blend in flour and allow to cook approximately 2 minutes, stirring often.
3. Gradually add 5½ cups of milk to the flour and oleo margarine mixture. Heat slowly, stirring constantly until mixture thickens.
4. Melt the remaining 1 tablespoon of oleo margarine in a small saucepan.
5. Add the diced celery and onions and sauté until tender.
6. Add the diced oysters and juice and simmer until tender, approximately 5 minutes or just until the edges curl, stirring gently.
7. Add salt and white pepper to taste.
8. Combine the oyster mixture to the thickened milk mixture.
9. Stir in cream.
10. If soup is not served immediately, hold soup *hot*, covered on a double-boiler set-up.

Note: Do not boil after oysters and cream are added.

Cheese Rolls, Glazed Apple Corn Bread Muffins, Cherry Muffins

BREADS, DRESSINGS

Breads and dressings is one of our largest categories, and many of these items are what we call Hot Shoppes signatures — unique flavors and appearances, which have cultivated a loyal following.

Our muffins have always had a distinctive look, because they're baked as mini-loaves, giving each one a slightly larger, soft crust. For simplicity's sake, the recipe included here calls for a conventional muffin tin, for circular muffins. However, a specialty cookware house will be able to provide you with a mini-loaf pan, if you wish to replicate exactly the Hot Shoppes muffin. Be careful, of course, to fill your baking tin only two-thirds of the way; too much, and you'll have a mess, too little, and you lose the "peak."

The simplest and shortest recipe in this section, Live Bread Crumbs, is as much responsible for Hot Shoppes' popularity as any of those that have received fanfare over the years. That's because we've always used Live Bread Crumbs for our fried entrees, and also for our prize-winning onion rings. For many years, every morning at all Hot Shoppes began with an employee switching on the "Buffalo Chopper" and making the Live Bread Crumbs to be used that day. And that day only. Our bread crumbs brown better, and more evenly. It's important to find a bread that yields the kind of bread crumbs you want, and to stick with it. Breads differ in amounts of dextrose, and one with too much will brown too quickly during baking. So the one that finally pleases you will have predictable amounts of this sugar, as well as yeast.

CHEESE ROLLS

Oleo Margarine	1 tablespoon
Shortening	1 tablespoon
Sugar, granulated	½ cup + 1 tablespoon
Cheddar Cheese, shredded	2 cups
Eggs, large	3 each
Yeast, dry	2 packets (¼ oz. each)
Water, lukewarm	½ cup
Flour, all purpose	6½–7 cups
Salt	2 teaspoons
Milk	1⅓ cups

YIELD: Approximately 3 to 4 dozen

PREPARATION:
1. Cream oleo margarine, shortening, sugar and shredded cheddar cheese until light.
2. Add eggs slowly, blending well between each addition.
3. Dissolve yeast in lukewarm water (be sure that water is not too hot).
4. Sift together flour and salt.
5. Add half of flour and half of milk to the cheese and egg mixture.
6. Add dissolved yeast.
7. Add remainder of milk and flour to make a soft dough.
8. Cover dough; let rest for 10 minutes.
9. Turn dough out onto a lightly floured surface and knead for 8 to 10 minutes or until dough is smooth and elastic.
10. Place dough in a lightly greased bowl large enough to hold dough when doubled in size, turning once to grease the surface.
11. Cover; let rise in a warm place (90°F) until double in size (about 2 hours).
12. Fold dough over from 4 sides. Let rise again until double in size.
13. Divide dough into 3 equal portions. Place each portion on a lightly floured surface. Round pieces by kneading until firm and smooth. Cover and let rest for 15 minutes.
14. Roll dough into a 12″ x 15″ elongated log approximately 3″ in diameter.
15. Cut each dough log into 12 to 14 equal portions depending on the size of roll desired. Shape into rolls as desired.
16. Place rolls in greased 13″ x 9″ x 2″ baking pans or muffin tins. Cover; let rise until almost double in size (about 45 minutes).
17. Bake in a preheated 350°F oven approximately 15 to 18 minutes or until done.
18. Brush tops with melted oleo margarine when removed from oven.
19. Keep warm until time of service.

NOTE:
— Yeast takes 5 to 10 minutes to soften. Follow manufacturer's directions for dissolving yeast.
— Generally, 1 package of dry yeast equals 0.6 oz. of cake compressed yeast.
— A heavy duty electric mixer may be used for mixing dough. Follow the directions given in the manufacturer's instruction booklet.

— If desired, Cheese Rolls may be baked individually in greased muffin pans.
— If desired, after Preparation Step #14, dough may be spread with additional oleo margarine and shredded cheddar cheese to enhance the flavor.
— If rolls are not served at once, they should be turned out of pans to cool.

Yeast grows best at a temperature between 80°F and 85°F. A high temperature will kill yeast; a low temperature will retard growth.

YEAST ROLLS

Oleo Margarine	4 tablespoons
Shortening	⅓ cup
Sugar, granulated	¾ cup + 1 tablespoon
Eggs, large	3 each
Yeast, active dry	4 packages (¼ oz. each)
Water, lukewarm	½ cup
Flour, all purpose	7½ cups
Salt	1 tablespoon
Milk	1¼ cups

YIELD: Approximately 4 to 4½ dozen

PREPARATION:
1. Cream oleo margarine and shortening with sugar until light.
2. Add eggs slowly, blending well between each addition.
3. Dissolve yeast in lukewarm water (be sure that water is not too hot).
4. Sift together flour and salt.
5. Add half of flour and half of milk to the shortening-sugar mixture.
6. Add dissolved yeast.
7. Add remainder of milk and flour to make a soft dough.
8. Cover dough; let rest for 10 minutes.
9. Turn dough out onto a lightly floured surface and knead for 8 to 10 minutes or until dough is smooth and elastic.
10. Place dough in a lightly greased bowl large enough to hold dough when doubled in size, turning once to grease the surface.
11. Cover; let rise in a warm place (90°F) until double in size (about 2 hours).
12. Fold dough over from 4 sides to knead lightly. Let rise again until double in size.
13. Turn dough out onto a lightly floured surface and shape as desired.

TO MAKE CLOVERLEAF ROLLS

1. Shape dough into small balls. Three balls should half-fill a greased muffin pan. Brush with melted oleo margarine or butter.
2. Let rise in a warm place (90°F) until double in size (about 25 to 30 minutes). Do not let rolls "over-rise".
3. Bake in a preheated 350°F oven until both the top and bottom of rolls are golden brown, about 10 to 12 minutes.
4. Remove from oven and brush top of rolls with melted oleo margarine.

TO MAKE PARKER HOUSE ROLLS

1. Roll dough ¼" to ½" thick on a lightly floured surface.
2. Cut dough with a floured 2½" round cutter; brush tops with soft oleo margarine or butter.
3. Make a crease (just off center) on the top of each circle of dough with the back of a knife.
4. Fold so that the top overlaps slightly; seal end edges.
5. Place on well-greased cookie sheets or 13"×9"×2" baking pans. Brush with melted oleo margarine or butter.
6. Let rolls rise until they are half again as large (about 45 minutes).
7. Bake in a preheated 350°F oven until golden brown, about 12 to 15 minutes.
8. Remove from oven and brush the tops of rolls with melted oleo margarine or butter.

NOTE:
— Yeast grows best at a temperature between 80°F and 85°F. A high temperature will kill yeast; a low temperature will retard growth.
— Yeast takes 5 to 10 minutes to soften. Follow manufacturer's directions for dissolving yeast.
— Generally, 1 package of dry yeast equals 0.6 oz. of cake compressed yeast.
— A heavy duty electric mixer may be used for mixing dough. Follow the directions given in the manufacturer's instruction booklet.

If rolls are not served at once, they should be turned out of pans to cool.

RUM BUNS

Butter or Oleo Margarine	2 tablespoons
Shortening	2 tablespoons
Sugar, granulated	4 tablespoons
Eggs, large	1 each
Yeast, active dry	1½ packets
Water, lukewarm	¼ cup
Flour, all purpose	2⅔ cups
Salt	1 teaspoon
Nutmeg, ground	¼ teaspoon
Milk	¼ cup
Rum Extract	1½ teaspoons
Raisins, lightly floured	3 tablespoons

Cinnamon Sugar Mixture

Cinnamon, ground	½ teaspoon
Sugar, granulated	2 tablespoons

Rum Syrup/Glaze

Water, heated to boiling	¼ cup
Sugar, granulated	⅓ cup
Rum Extract	¼ teaspoon

Rum Frosting

Sugar, confectioners	6 tablespoons
Butter or Oleo Margarine	1 tablespoon
Rum Extract	¼ teaspoon
Karo Syrup, white	¼ teaspoon
Milk or Half and Half	1 tablespoon

YIELD:	Approximately 1 dozen

PREPARATION:

1. Cream butter or oleo margarine and shortening until smooth.
2. Add sugar and continue to cream until light in color and sugar is completely dissolved.
3. Add egg, beating slowly until well blended.
4. Dissolve yeast in lukewarm water (be sure that water is not too hot).
5. Sift together flour, salt and nutmeg to blend well. Add half of flour to the margarine/sugar/egg mixture and mix until thoroughly combined.
6. Add dissolved yeast mixture.
7. Stir rum extract into the milk to blend.
8. Add remaining flour and then the milk mixture and beat until smooth.
9. Add lightly floured raisins and mix to blend uniformly.
10. Place dough in a lightly greased bowl (large enough to hold the dough when doubled in size), turning once to grease the surface.

11. Cover; let rise in a warm place (90°F) until double in size (about 2 hours).
12. Place dough on a lightly floured surface.
13. Fold dough over from four sides to knead lightly and then return dough to bowl. Let rise again until double in size.
14. Turn dough out onto a lightly floured surface and shape into a smooth, firm mound.
15. Cover and let rest for 10 minutes.
16. Roll dough into 12″ × 15″ rectangular shape that is approximately ½″ in height.
17. Spread or brush surface with softened butter or oleo margarine.
18. Combine cinnamon and sugar and mix well.
19. Sprinkle cinnamon sugar mixture over surface of dough, leaving approximately 1″ clear along one of the 12″ sides.
20. Roll dough tightly along the 15″ side. The finished roll should be 12″ in length.
21. Cut dough into 12 even slices.
22. Place rolls cut side down in a greased 13″ × 9″ × 2″ baking pan with each roll almost touching each other.
23. Brush rolls with melted butter or oleo margarine. Cover; let rise in a warm place (90°F) until almost double in size (about 45 minutes).
24. Bake in a preheated 375°F oven approximately 15 to 18 minutes or until done.
25. Remove from oven and brush while still hot with the Rum Syrup which will be partially absorbed.
26. TO MAKE RUM SYRUP/GLAZE:
    — Add sugar to boiling water and heat over low heat until sugar is dissolved completely and mixture becomes syrupy.
    — Hold warm over hot water, if necessary, until needed to brush over rolls.

Rum Buns

27. When rolls have cooled slightly, but are still warm, spread Rum Frosting evenly over the surface of each roll.
28. TO MAKE RUM FROSTING:
    - Sift confectioners sugar before measuring.
    - Cream sugar and butter or oleo margarine together until light and fluffy.
    - Blend in Karo Syrup, milk, and rum extract.
    - Hold at room temperature until needed to frost rolls.
29. Hold rolls warm until time of service.

NOTE:
- Yeast grows best at a temperature between 80°F and 85°F. A high temperature will kill yeast; a low temperature will retard growth.
- Yeast takes 5 to 10 minutes to soften. Follow manufacturer's directions for dissolving yeast.
- Generally, 1 package of dry yeast equals 0.6 oz. of cake compressed yeast.
- If rolls are not served at once, they should be turned out of pans to cool.
- A heavy duty electric mixer may be used for mixing dough. Follow the directions given in the manufacturer's booklet.

HOT CROSS BUNS

Nutmeg, ground	*1 teaspoon*
Mace, ground	*1 teaspoon*
Cinnamon, ground	*1 teaspoon*
Sugar, granulated	*1 cup*
Butter or Oleo Margarine	*4 tablespoons*
Shortening	*4 tablespoons*
Eggs, large	*3 each*
Yeast, active dry	*6 packets*
Water, lukewarm	*½ cup*
Flour, all purpose	*8 cups*
Salt	*1 tablespoon*
Milk	*2 cups*
Currants	*¾ cup*
Mixed Citron or Glace Fruit, ¼" dice	*1½ cups*
Sugar, confectioners	*1½ cups*
Sugar, granulated	*¼ cup*
Water	*⅛ cup*
Butter or Oleo Margarine	*2½ tablespoons*
YIELD:	*Approximately 4 to 5 dozen*

PREPARATION:
1. Combine spices with sugar and stir until well-blended.
2. Cream together butter or oleo margarine with shortening.
3. Add the spice/sugar mixture and continue blending until thoroughly combined.
4. Add eggs slowly, blending well between each addition.
5. Dissolve yeast in lukewarm water (be sure that water is not too hot).
6. Sift together flour and salt.
7. Combine 4 cups of flour with egg mixture and 1 cup of milk.
8. Add dissolved yeast to the mixture then add remaining flour and 2nd cup of milk and continue blending until a soft dough is formed.
9. Wash currants and drain thoroughly.
10. Mix diced fruit with currants and add until fruits are evenly distributed throughout the dough.
11. Place dough in a lightly greased bowl (large enough to hold the dough when doubled in size), turning once to grease the surface.
12. Cover; let rise in a warm place (90° F) until double in size (about 2 hours).
13. Place dough on a lightly floured surface.
14. Divide dough into three even pieces; cover and let rest for 10 minutes.
15. Cut each piece into 20 portions and shape into rounded buns.
16. Place buns in greased 13″ × 9″ × 2″ baking pans or baking sheets.
17. Cover; let rise in a warm place (90° F) until almost double in size (about 45 minutes).
18. Bake in a preheated 350° F oven approximately 15 minutes or until done. Cool slightly.
19. TO MAKE FROSTING:
    — Sift confectioner's sugar before measuring.
    — Cream sugars with butter and add water gradually until frosting is smooth and well blended.
20. Using a pastry bag, pipe frosting on top of each cooled bun to form a cross.

NOTE:
— Yeast grows best at a temperature between 80° F and 85° F. A high temperature will kill yeast; a low temperature will retard growth.
— Yeast takes 5 to 10 minutes to soften. Follow manufacturer's directions for dissolving yeast.
— Generally, 1 package of dry yeast equals 0.6 oz. of cake compressed yeast.
— If rolls are not served at once, they should be turned out of pans to cool.
— A heavy duty electric mixer may be used for mixing dough. Follow the directions given in the manufacturer's instruction booklet.

BUTTERMILK BISCUITS

Flour, all purpose	*2⅓ cups*
Baking Powder, double acting	*1 tablespoon +*
	2 teaspoons
Baking Soda	*½ teaspoon*
Salt	*½ teaspoon*
Shortening	*1 cup*
Buttermilk	*¾ cup*
YIELD:	*12 each 2½″ biscuits*

PREPARATION:
1. Sift together flour, baking powder, baking soda and salt.
2. Cut in shortening until mixture resembles coarse crumbs.
3. Add buttermilk all at once, stirring only until dough follows fork around the bowl.
4. Turn out on a lightly floured surface and knead gently for ½ minute.
5. Roll ½″ to ¾″ thick; cut with a floured 2½″ biscuit cutter.
6. Place biscuits on a lightly greased baking tray about 1″ apart for slightly crusty biscuits.
7. Bake in a preheated 450°F oven for approximately 12 to 15 minutes or until golden brown.

NOTE:
— If biscuits with softer sides are desired, place them close together with sides touching on a shallow baking pan or cookie sheet.

Uneven distribution of baking powder and soda will result in yellow or brown flecks on the top surface of baked biscuits.

LIVE BREAD CRUMBS

PREPARATION:
1. Use day-old bread.
2. Place bread in mixing bowl of a *heavy duty* mixer and mix with a wire beater on low speed until fine crumbs are formed.
3. Hold crumbs in a tightly closed plastic bag in the refrigerator until used.

NOTE:
— If a heavy duty mixer is not available, bread may be finely grated on a hand held grater.

BUTTERED CRUMBS AND CHEESE CRUMB TOPPING

Buttered Crumb Topping

Bread Crumbs—*from day old bread*	2 cups
Oleo Margarine	4 tablespoons
YIELD:	Approximately 2 cups

Cheese Crumb Topping

Bread Crumbs—*from day old bread*	2 cups
Oleo Margarine	4 tablespoons
Sharp Cheese, *finely shredded*	½ pound (2 cups)
YIELD:	Approximately 3 to 4 cups

PREPARATION:
1. Work oleo margarine into the bread crumbs until oleo is the size of peas.
2. For Cheese Crumb Topping: add the finely shredded sharp cheese to buttered crumbs. Blend well.
3. Use Cheese Crumb Topping as desired to garnish casseroles. Top casserole with Cheese Crumbs according to recipe instructions.
4. For Browned Butter Crumbs:
   — Place buttered crumbs on a flat cookie sheet or baking tray.
   — Place tray in a preheated 350° F oven and heat until crumbs are a golden brown—approximately 15 minutes.
   — Stir crumbs at least three times while browning to allow crumbs to brown evenly.
   — Use to garnish casseroles as desired or according to instructions listed on individual recipes.
   — Browned Butter Crumbs may also be used for items not cooked in the oven.

CHEESE TOPPING FOR AU GRATIN ITEMS

Flour, all purpose	2 tablespoons + 2 teaspoons
Paprika	½ teaspoon
Oleo Margarine, *well-chilled*	2 tablespoons
Sharp Cheddar Cheese, *shredded*	⅔ cup
YIELD:	Approximately ¾ cup

PREPARATION:
1. Mix flour with paprika.
2. Combine shredded cheese, well-chilled oleo margarine and flour mixture *just* until crumbly. If overworked, the mixture will form a paste.
3. Use as desired to top Au Gratin dishes prior to baking.

SEASONED CROUTONS

Oleo Margarine, softened	*½ cup*
Parmesan Cheese	*⅓ cup*
Parsley, finely chopped	*2 tablespoons*
White Bread, slices	*7 each*
YIELD:	*6 to 8 servings*

PREPARATION:
1. Place softened oleo margarine in a medium-size mixing bowl. Add the parmesan cheese and finely chopped parsley. Mix well to combine, using a rubber spatula, rotary or electric mixer.
2. Remove crusts from bread. Spread each slice of white bread with oleo-cheese mixture, spreading evenly to corners.
3. Cut each slice diagonally into 4 pieces.
4. Place on greased cookie sheet. Bake in a preheated 250°F oven for approximately 40 minutes until croutons are dry and golden brown.

NOTE:
— Croutons may be prepared up to 2 hours in advance.

Croutons may be used as a garnish on soups or specialty salads.

CHEESE CROUTONS

Oleo Margarine	*4 tablespoons*
Sharp Cheddar Cheese, grated	*½ cup*
White Bread, slices	*7 each*
YIELD:	*6 to 8 servings*

PREPARATION:
1. Place softened oleo margarine in a medium-size mixing bowl. Add the grated Cheddar cheese. Cream together until very light.
2. Remove crusts from bread. Spread each slice of white bread with oleo-cheese mixture, spreading evenly to corners.
3. Place whole slices on a greased cookie sheet and heat in a preheated 325°F oven until cheese is almost melted.
4. Cool to facilitate cutting into ½" pieces. Cut each slice of bread four across by four down to yield 16-½" cubes per slice.
5. Using a pie spatula, place cubes on cookie sheet and return to oven until lightly brown on top.

NOTE:
— For Cheese Triangles: Follow preparation for croutons above through Preparation Step #3. Cut each slice of bread in 4 triangles. Finish baking until croutons are lightly browned and crisp.

FRICASSEE DUMPLINGS

Flour, all purpose	*¾ cup*
Baking Powder, double acting	*1 teaspoon*
Salt	*¼ teaspoon*
Milk	*½ cup*
Oleo Margarine	*1 tablespoon*
YIELD:	*6 to 8 servings*

PREPARATION:
1. Sift together flour, baking powder and salt.
2. Cut in oleo margarine until mixture resembles coarse crumbs.
3. Add milk, stirring just until moistened.
4. Drop from a tablespoon on top of a bubbling stew.
5. Cover tightly; bring to a boil. Reduce heat (don't lift cover).
6. Simmer 12 to 15 minutes or until done.

TO COOK DUMPLINGS IN FRICASSEE SAUCE
— Place one quart of boiling Fricassee Sauce in a two quart baking pan.
— Place dumplings on top of the boiling sauce using a level tablespoon.
— Cover tightly with foil and bake for 20 minutes in a preheated 350°F oven.

NOTE:
— Dumplings may be served with chicken, lamb, giblets or as desired.

BREAD DRESSING

White Bread, sliced	*20 slices*
Onion, ¼″ dice	*1 ½ cups*
Celery, ¼″ dice	*1 ⅔ cups*
Oleo Margarine	*1 cup*
Poultry Seasoning	*1 tablespoon*
Chicken Base	*2 tablespoons*
White Pepper	*⅛ teaspoon*
YIELD:	*6 to 8 servings*

PREPARATION:
1. Cut bread slices to make small cubes, approximately ½″ × ½″.
2. Dice onion and celery into ¼″ pieces.
3. Sauté vegetables until tender in oleo margarine.
4. Remove from heat. Add poultry seasoning, chicken base and white pepper.
5. Combine sautéed vegetable mixture with cubed bread.
6. Toss gently to mix.
7. Place in a greased 8″ × 8″ baking pan, pressing lightly into pan.
8. Cover with aluminum foil and seal around the edges, leaving one end loose.
9. Bake in a preheated 350°F oven for 35 to 40 minutes or until thoroughly heated.

NOTE:
— Keep dressing covered with foil to prevent drying out.
— If desired, dressing may be used to stuff a 4 to 5 pound chicken or capon.
— To stuff a 10 pound turkey, the recipe will need to be doubled.

CORN BREAD DRESSING

Onion, ¼″ dice	*½ cup*
Celery, ¼″ dice	*½ cup*
Oleo Margarine	*1 tablespoon*
Corn Bread	*2 ¾ cups*
Poultry Seasoning	*½ teaspoon*
Water	*1 cup*
Chicken Base	*1 tablespoon*
YIELD:	*6 to 8 servings*

PREPARATION:
1. Sauté onion and celery in oleo margarine.
2. Break corn bread into approximately ⅜″ pieces.

3. Add poultry seasoning to corn bread and toss lightly to mix evenly.
4. Add sautéed onion and celery. Mix lightly.
5. Dissolve chicken base in water. Add to mixture and toss lightly.
6. Place stuffing in a greased casserole dish or baking pan.
7. Bake in a preheated 350° F oven until heated thoroughly and lightly browned, approximately 30 to 35 minutes.

NOTE:
— If desired, cornbread dressing may be used to stuff a 3 to 4 pound chicken just before roasting.
— For stuffing a larger chicken or turkey, it will be necessary to double or triple this recipe to yield the desired quantity depending on the size of the bird.

If a moister dressing is desired, cover dish/pan with aluminum foil prior to baking.

DRESSING FOR STUFFED FISH

Bread, ¼" dice	*4 cups*
Onions, ¼" dice	*⅞ cup*
Celery, ¼" dice	*1 cup*
Oleo Margarine	*8 tablespoons*
Dill Pickle — drained thoroughly and finely chopped	*½ cup + 1 tablespoon*
Poultry Seasoning	*1 tablespoon*
Chicken Base	*1½ tablespoons*
White Pepper	*To Taste*
YIELD:	*6 to 8 servings*

PREPARATION:
1. Dice bread into ¼" cubes.
2. Dice the onions and celery into ¼" pieces and sauté in the oleo margarine until tender.
3. Add seasoning and chicken base to sautéed onions and celery; stir well to blend and remove from heat.
4. Combine the cooked vegetables and finely chopped pickle with the bread cubes.
5. Toss gently to mix; do not mash.
6. Use as directed for Baked Stuffed Fillet of Fish.

SPOON BREAD

Eggs, large	*4 each*
Sugar, granulated	*⅓ cup*
Oleo Margarine	*¾ cup*
Milk	*3¼ cups*
Salt	*1 teaspoon*
Yellow Corn Meal	*⅔ cup + 1 tablespoon*
YIELD:	*6 to 8 servings*

PREPARATION:
1. Place eggs and sugar in mixing bowl. Beat until eggs double their volume.
2. Melt oleo margarine in a medium-size sauce pan over low heat. Add milk and heat to approximately 200°F (just below the boiling point). Add salt and blend well.
3. Slowly add corn meal, stirring constantly with a hand whip or rotary mixer for 4 to 5 minutes. Mixture will be VERY thick.
4. Remove from heat.
5. Fold beaten eggs into corn meal mixture using a hand wire whip.
6. Pour mixture into a greased 2 quart baking pan.
7. Set baking pan inside a shallow pan on oven rack. Pour hot water around baking pan, 1" deep.
8. Bake in a preheated 350°F oven for approximately 1¼ hours — until golden brown or until a knife inserted in the center comes out clean.

HUSH PUPPIES

DRY MIXTURE:

Yellow Cornmeal	*⅞ cup*
Flour, all purpose	*⅓ cup + 2 tablespoons*
Baking Soda	*½ teaspoon*
Baking Powder, double acting	*1½ tablespoons*
Salt	*½ teaspoon*

WET MIXTURE:

Egg, small — beaten	*1 each*
Onions, minced	*¼ cup*
Buttermilk	*1 cup*
YIELD:	*6 to 8 servings*

PREPARATION:
1. Sift together dry ingredients into a medium-size mixing bowl: cornmeal, flour, baking soda, baking powder and salt.

2. To dry mixture add beaten egg, minced onion and buttermilk. Mix well, but just until moistened.
3. Drop batter in heaping teaspoonfuls into a preheated 350° F deep fat fryer.
4. Fry hush puppies until puffy and golden brown on all sides, approximately 3 to 4 minutes, depending on the make and model of deep fryer used.
5. Remove hush puppies from fryer and drain on paper towels.
6. Serve with fish and seafood menu items or as desired.

CORN BREAD/CORN STICKS

Yellow Corn Meal	*1½ cups*
Flour, all purpose	*1¼ cups*
Soft Shortening	*½ cup + 2 tablespoons*
Baking Powder, double acting	*1 teaspoon*
Baking Soda	*½ teaspoon*
Salt	*½ teaspoon*
Sugar, granulated	*⅓ cup*
Eggs, large	*3 each*
Buttermilk	*2 cups*
YIELD:	*6 to 8 servings*

PREPARATION:
1. Sift corn meal, flour, salt, baking powder and soda together.
2. Blend shortening with the dry ingredients until mixture has a mealy appearance.
3. Add sugar and mix to blend.
4. In a medium-size mixing bowl, beat eggs with a wire whip or rotary or electric mixer until light and smooth, about 1 minute.
5. Add buttermilk and blend with egg.
6. Add dry mixture to the egg and buttermilk mixture and mix just to blend. DO NOT OVER BEAT.
7. Pour mixture into a preheated, greased and floured 9″ × 9″ × 2″ pan.
8. Bake in a preheated 425° F oven for 25 to 30 minutes until golden brown.

NOTE:
For Corn Bread Sticks
— Spoon prepared batter into preheated, greased corn stick pans, filling ⅔ full. Bake in a preheated 425° F oven for 12 to 15 minutes or until golden brown. Remove corn sticks from pan while still warm.

PLAIN, RAISIN OR NUT MUFFINS

Flour, all purpose	*1¾ cups*
Salt	*½ teaspoon*
Baking Powder, double acting	*1 tablespoon + 1 teaspoon*
Oleo Margarine	*4 tablespoons + 2 teaspoons*
Shortening	*2 tablespoons*
Sugar, granulated	*⅓ cup + 1 tablespoon*
Eggs, large	*2 each*
Milk	*1 cup*
Raisins or Nuts – if desired	*1 cup*
YIELD:	*Approximately 12 each*

PREPARATION:
1. Sift flour, salt and baking powder into mixing bowl.
2. Cut in firm oleo margarine and shortening until mixture resembles coarse crumbs. Ingredients must be well-mixed.
3. Add sugar and blend well.
4. In a separate mixing bowl, beat eggs until light.
5. Add milk to the beaten eggs and stir well to blend.
6. Combine dry muffin mixture with the egg-milk mixture and stir quickly just until dry ingredients are moistened.
7. Place batter in greased and floured muffin pans or paper baking cups filling pans ⅔ full.
8. Bake in a preheated 350°F oven until golden brown, approximately 20 to 25 minutes.
9. Remove muffins from pan while still warm.

NOTE:
— For Raisin Muffins: Wash raisins, drain thoroughly, and dust with flour. Stir gently into the muffin batter after Preparation Step #6.
— For Nut Muffins: Dust coarsely chopped nuts with flour. Stir gently into the muffin batter after Preparation Step #6.

BLUEBERRY MUFFINS

Flour, all purpose	1¾ cups
Salt	½ teaspoon
Baking Powder, double acting	1 tablespoon + 1 teaspoon
Oleo Margarine	4 tablespoons + 2 teaspoons
Shortening	2 tablespoons
Sugar, granulated	⅓ cup + 1 tablespoon
Eggs, large	2 each
Milk	1 cup
Blueberries, fresh or well-drained, frozen	1 cup
Flour, all purpose	¼ cup

YIELD: Approximately 12 each

PREPARATION:
1. Sift and blend flour, salt and baking powder into mixing bowl.
2. Cut in firm oleo margarine and shortening until mixture resembles coarse crumbs. Ingredients must be well mixed.
3. Add sugar and blend well.
4. In a separate mixing bowl, beat eggs until light.
5. Add milk to beaten egg and stir well to blend.
6. Combine the dry muffin mixture with the egg-milk mixture and stir quickly just until dry ingredients are moistened.
7. To 1 cup fresh or well-drained frozen blueberries, add ¼ cup all-purpose flour. Gently toss blueberries with flour to coat all sides.
8. Stir flour-coated blueberries gently into muffin batter.
9. Place batter in greased and floured muffin tins or paper baking cups, filling ⅔ full.
10. Bake in a preheated 350° F oven until golden brown, approximately 20 to 25 minutes.
11. Remove muffins from pan while still warm.

BANANA MUFFINS

Flour, all purpose	1 ¾ cups
Salt	½ teaspoon
Baking Powder, double acting	1 tablespoon + 1 teaspoon
Oleo Margarine	4 tablespoons + 2 teaspoons
Shortening	2 tablespoons
Sugar, granulated	⅓ cup + 1 tablespoon
Eggs, large	2 each
Milk	⅔ cup
Banana, ripe—mashed	1 cup

YIELD: Approximately 12 each

PREPARATION:
1. Sift and blend flour, salt and baking powder into mixing bowl.
2. Cut in firm oleo margarine and shortening until mixture resembles course crumbs. Ingredients must be well mixed.
3. Add sugar and blend well.
4. In a separate mixing bowl, beat eggs until foamy. Add milk and mashed bananas. Blend thoroughly.
5. Combine dry muffin mixture with the egg-milk-banana mixture. Blend just until dry ingredients are moistened, but still lumpy. DO NOT OVER MIX.
6. Place batter in greased and floured muffin tins or paper baking cups, filling pans ⅔ full.
7. Bake in a preheated 400° F oven until golden brown, approximately 20 to 25 minutes.
8. Remove muffins from pan while still warm.

CHERRY MUFFINS

Flour, all purpose	1 ¾ cups
Salt	½ teaspoon
Baking Powder, double acting	1 tablespoon + 1 teaspoon
Oleo Margarine	4 tablespoons + 2 teaspoons
Shortening	2 tablespoons
Sugar, granulated	⅓ cup + 1 tablespoon
Eggs, large	2 each
Milk	1 cup
Cherries, drained	1 cup
YIELD:	Approximately 12 each

PREPARATION:
1. Sift and blend flour, salt and baking powder into mixing bowl.
2. Cut in firm oleo margarine and shortening until mixture resembles coarse crumbs. Ingredients must be well-mixed.
3. Add sugar and blend well.
4. In a separate mixing bowl, beat eggs until light.
5. Add milk to the beaten eggs and stir well to blend.
6. Combine dry muffin mixture with the egg-milk mixture and stir quickly just until dry ingredients are moistened.
7. Stir *drained* cherries gently into muffin batter.

8. Place batter in greased and floured muffin tins or paper baking cups, filling pans ⅔ full.
9. Bake in a preheated 350° F oven until golden brown, approximately 20 to 25 minutes.
10. Remove muffins from pan while still warm.

PINEAPPLE MUFFINS

Flour, all purpose	*1¾ cups*
Salt	*½ teaspoon*
Baking Powder, double acting	*1 tablespoon + 1 teaspoon*
Oleo Margarine	*4 tablespoons + 2 teaspoons*
Shortening	*2 tablespoons*
Sugar, granulated	*⅓ cup + 1 tablespoon*
Eggs, large	*2 each*
Juice plus Milk	*¾ cup*
Pineapple, crushed — drained with juice reserved	*¾ cup*

YIELD: *Approximately 12 each*

PREPARATION:
1. Sift and blend flour, salt and baking powder into mixing bowl.
2. Cut in firm oleo margarine and shortening until mixture resembles coarse crumbs. Ingredients must be well-mixed.
3. Add sugar and blend well.
4. In a separate mixing bowl, beat eggs until foamy.
5. Measure juice from drained pineapple. Add milk to measure ¾ cup combined liquid and add to eggs, mixing just until combined.
6. Add well-drained crushed pineapple all at once to muffin batter, folding gently until blended.
7. Place muffin batter in greased and floured muffin tins or paper baking cups, filling ⅔ full.
8. Bake in a preheated 350° F oven until golden brown, approximately 20 to 25 minutes.

Note: Remove muffins from pan while still warm.

SPICE MUFFINS

Flour, all purpose	1 ¾ cups
Salt	½ teaspoon
Baking Powder, double acting	1 tablespoon + 1 teaspoon
Oleo Margarine	4 tablespoons + 2 teaspoons
Shortening	2 tablespoons
Sugar, granulated	⅓ cup + 1 tablespoon
Eggs, large	2 each
Water, cold	⅓ cup + 1 tablespoon
Molasses	⅓ cup + 1 tablespoon
Cloves, ground	¼ teaspoon
Ginger, ground	½ teaspoon
Cinnamon	½ teaspoon

YIELD: *Approximately 12 each*

PREPARATION:
1. Sift and blend flour, salt and baking powder into mixing bowl.
2. Cut in firm oleo margarine and shortening until mixture resembles coarse crumbs. Ingredients must be well mixed.
3. Add sugar and blend well.
4. In a separate mixing bowl, beat eggs and cold water on medium speed of electric mixer for 1 minute.
5. Combine dry muffin mixture with the egg-water mixture and continue to blend for an additional 2 minutes. Scrape bowl and beaters.
6. Add molasses, cinnamon, ginger and cloves and mix until well blended.
7. Place batter in greased and floured muffin tins or paper baking cups, filling pans ⅔ full.
8. Bake in a preheated 400° F oven until golden brown and firm on top, approximately 20 to 25 minutes.
9. Remove muffins from pan while still warm.

PUMPKIN MUFFINS

Flour, all purpose	1 ⅔ cups
Baking Powder, double acting	1 tablespoon
Salt	½ teaspoon
Baking Soda	⅓ teaspoon
Cinnamon, ground	2 teaspoons
Nutmeg	1 ½ teaspoons
Sugar, granulated	¾ cups
Oleo Margarine	5 tablespoons + 1 teaspoon
Pumpkin, canned or mashed cooked	½ cup
Milk	¾ cup
Eggs, large	3 each
Raisins, seedless	¾ cup

YIELD: Approximately 12 each

PREPARATION:
1. Wash raisins and drain. Dredge with a small amount of the measured flour before mixing with the other dry ingredients.
2. Sift together flour, baking powder, salt, baking soda, cinnamon, nutmeg and sugar.
3. Add oleo margarine and beat on low speed of electric mixer for approximately 3 minutes.
4. Add pumpkin to the milk and add slowly to the flour mixture, beating continuously while adding.
5. Continue beating about 4 minutes until light and smooth.
6. Add eggs one at a time beating 1 minute after each addition.
7. Add flour-coated raisins and mix just until blended.
8. Place muffin batter in greased and floured muffin tins or paper baking cups, filling ⅔ full.
9. Bake in a preheated 350°F oven until golden brown, approximately 20 to 25 minutes.
10. Remove muffins from pan while still warm.

BRAN MUFFINS

Flour, all purpose	*1 cup + 3 tablespoons*
Baking Powder, double acting	*2 teaspoons*
Salt	*¼ teaspoon*
Baking Soda	*1 teaspoon*
Whole Bran (unprocessed)	*1 ½ cups*
Sugar, granulated	*½ cup*
Oleo Margarine, firm	*6 ½ tablespoons*
Buttermilk	*1 ½ cups*
Eggs, large	*2 each*
Molasses	*¼ cup*

YIELD: *Approximately 12 to 15 each*

PREPARATION:
1. Sift together flour, baking powder, salt and baking soda. Stir in bran.
2. Add sugar and firm oleo margarine.
3. Cut in oleo margarine until mixture is mealy.
4. Beat eggs slightly; add buttermilk and molasses. Stir to combine.
5. Combine dry ingredient mixture with liquid ingredients, stirring *just until moistened*.
6. Place batter in greased and floured muffin tins or paper baking cups, filling ⅔ full.
7. Bake in a preheated 400°F oven until golden brown, approximately 15 to 20 minutes.
8. Remove muffins from pan while still warm.

NOTE:
— For variation, ½ to ¾ cup of seedless raisins, coarsely chopped nuts or coarsely cut dates may be added to the batter prior to baking. Lightly dust these ingredients with flour to prevent them from sinking to the bottom of the muffins during the baking process.

SPICED APPLE MUFFINS

Flour, all purpose	*2 cups*
Salt	*¼ teaspoon*
Baking Powder, double acting	*2 teaspoons*
Baking Soda	*½ teaspoon*
Cinnamon	*2 teaspoons*
Sugar, granulated	*½ cup*
Nutmeg	*1 ½ teaspoons*
Oleo Margarine	*5 tablespoons + 1 teaspoon*
Apples, cored & peeled — ¼ " dice	*1 cup*
Milk	*⅔ cup*
Eggs, large	*2 each*
YIELD:	*Approximately 12 to 15 muffins*

PREPARATION:
1. Sift all dry ingredients into a medium size mixing bowl.
2. Add oleo margarine to dry ingredients and mix on low speed of electric mixer until mixture has a mealy appearance.
3. Add milk and beat for approximately 30 seconds.
4. Add eggs, one at a time, beating approximately 30 seconds after each addition.
5. Add finely chopped apples and mix on lowest speed just enough to blend.
6. Fill greased muffin pans or paper baking cups ⅔ full.
7. Bake in a preheated 350°F oven for 20 to 25 minutes until muffins are light golden brown and baked thoroughly.
8. Remove muffins from pan while still warm.

GLAZED APPLE CORN BREAD MUFFINS

Yellow Corn Meal	*1 ½ cups*
Flour, all purpose	*1 ¼ cups*
Salt	*½ teaspoon*
Baking Powder, double acting	*1 tablespoon*
Baking Soda	*½ teaspoon*
Shortening	*½ cup + 2 tablespoons*
Sugar, granulated	*⅓ cup*
Eggs, large	*3 each*
Buttermilk	*2 cups*
Apples, cored & peeled — ¼ " dice	*2 cups*
Honey (to glaze)	*4 tablespoons*
YIELD:	*Approximately 12 to 15 muffins*

PREPARATION:
1. Sift cornmeal, flour, salt, baking powder and soda together.
2. Blend shortening with dry ingredients until mixture has a mealy appearance.
3. Add sugar and mix to blend.
4. In a medium-size mixing bowl, beat eggs with a wire whip or rotary or electric mixer until light and smooth, about 1 minute.
5. Add buttermilk and blend with eggs.
6. Combine diced apples with the egg mixture.
7. Add dry mixture to the egg and buttermilk mixture and mix just to blend, but still lumpy.
8. Fill greased muffin pans or paper baking cups ⅔ full.
9. Bake in a preheated 350°F oven for 20–25 minutes until muffins are light golden brown and baked thoroughly.
10. Remove muffins from pan while still warm.
11. Glaze each muffin with honey by drizzling ⅓ teaspoon over each warm muffin.

NOTE:
— Hold baked and glazed muffins in a roll warmer or heated roll basket, single layer, for up to ½ hour only. Stacking muffins will remove glaze.

Muffins should be baked as close to service as possible.

Creole Sauce on Scrambled Eggs

SAUCES, GRAVIES

Depending upon which dictionary you believe, "barbeque" derives from a word that means "a framework of sticks" or from a word that means "from beard-to-tail" (in French, "barbe-a-queue"). Either way, the meat gets cooked. And either way, barbeque sauce is one of the essential elements of the Hot Shoppes legacy.

There are actually far more barbeque sauces than there are spellings or definitions of the word. The Southwestern is sweeter and thicker, with more tomato base, but south of the border the barbeque is hotter and thinner, with more cayenne pepper. Both of these flavors, and others, have influenced the Hot Shoppes; as a young man, Bill Marriott was introduced to these flavors while herding sheep and cattle with both Mexicans and Southwesterners.

Even with these many sources, however, the barbeque sauce we make at the Hot Shoppes has been extremely consistent over the years, because our customers wouldn't let us swerve. So to have a genuine Hot Shoppes barbeque, follow our sauce recipes closely, and then mix the various sauces together in the recommended proportions—for example, our barbeque beef sandwich calls for equal parts St. Louis Sauce and Barbeque Sauce.

Once you've mastered our Hot Shoppes sauces, you can create interesting variety by applying them in new combinations, and with different ingredients. The Creole Sauce, for instance, works well with almost every part of the chicken, including the eggs. And the Mighty Mo sauce is a great topping for a range of delicatessen style sandwiches.

LEMON BUTTER

Oleo Margarine or Butter	*½ cup*
Onion, minced	*1 teaspoon*
Lemon Juice	*1 tablespoon*
Salt	*½ teaspoon*
White Pepper	*¼ teaspoon*
YIELD:	*6 to 8 portions*

PREPARATION:
1. Hold oleo margarine or butter at room temperature until softened.
   DO NOT MELT.
2. Cream oleo margarine slowly, adding the lemon juice, minced onion, salt and white pepper.
3. Mix until all the liquid is absorbed.
4. Place approximately ½ tablespoon of lemon butter on top of each portion of raw fish prior to baking.

NOTE:
— For Parslied Lemon Butter, sprinkle fish with finely chopped fresh parsley at time of service.

HORSERADISH SOUR CREAM SAUCE

Sour Cream	*1 cup*
Horseradish, prepared	*1 tablespoon + 1 teaspoon*
Salt	*¼ teaspoon*
White Pepper	*⅛ teaspoon*
YIELD:	*6 to 8 servings*

PREPARATION:
1. Combine all ingredients; blend well.
2. Store in a tightly covered container under refrigeration until time of service.
3. Serve as desired or as an accompaniment to roast beef.

COCKTAIL SAUCE

Catsup	¾ cup
Worcestershire Sauce	½ teaspoon
Tabasco Sauce	4 drops
Horseradish, prepared	1 tablespoon
Salt	⅛ teaspoon
Water	¼ cup
YIELD:	6 to 8 servings

PREPARATION:
1. Combine all ingredients; blend well.
2. Store in a tightly covered container under refrigeration until time of service.
3. Serve as desired or as an accompaniment to steamed or deep fried shrimp or seafood cocktails.

MIGHTY MO SAUCE

Catsup	½ cup
Chili Sauce	¼ cup
A-1 Sauce	1½ teaspoons
Worcestershire Sauce	½ teaspoon
Tabasco Sauce	2 drops
Sweet Pickle, finely chopped	½ cup
Mayonnaise	1¼ cups
YIELD:	2½ cups

PREPARATION:
1. Combine catsup, chili sauce, A-1 Sauce, Worcestershire sauce and Tabasco Sauce.
2. Finely chop sweet pickles and add to the sauce mixture.
3. Combine the sauce/pickle mixture with mayonnaise, stirring until well-blended.

Note: Store in a tightly covered container under refrigeration until time of service.

CRANBERRY SAUCE

Sugar, granulated	2 cups
Water	1½ cups
Cranberries, fresh	1 pound (4 cups)
YIELD:	5 cups

PREPARATION:
1. Combine sugar and water in sauce pan; stir to dissolve sugar.
2. Heat to boiling; boil 5 minutes.
3. Add cranberries and cook until the skins "pop", approximately 5 minutes.
4. Remove from heat.
5. Serve sauce warm or chilled as a meat accompaniment or relish.

CELERY SAUCE

Tomatoes, canned—drained	2¾ cups
Onion, ¼ " dice	¾ cup
Sugar, granulated	¼ cup
Vinegar, cider	⅓ cup + 1 tablespoon
Green Pepper, ¼ " dice	⅓ cup + 1 tablespoon
Celery, ¼ " dice	2½ cups
Salt	To Taste
White Pepper	To Taste
Mustard Seed	2 tablespoons + 1 teaspoon
Horseradish, prepared	1 teaspoon
YIELD:	Approximately 4 cups

PREPARATION:
1. Thoroughly drain and chop tomatoes into ½ " pieces.
2. Combine all ingredients, except mustard seed and horseradish, and simmer for approximately 20 minutes, leaving vegetables crisp.
3. Remove from heat and add mustard seed and horseradish. Stir well to blend.
4. Cool and store in a tightly covered container under refrigeration until time of service.
5. Serve as desired or as an accompaniment with hot dogs.

HOT SAUCE

Catsup	½ cup
Water	¾ cup
Tabasco Sauce	1¼ teaspoons
Dry Mustard	2 teaspoons
Worcestershire Sauce	1½ teaspoons
YIELD:	Approximately 1 cup

PREPARATION:
1. Combine all ingredients and blend well.
2. Store in a tightly covered container under refrigeration until time of service.
3. Serve as an accompaniment with the Barbeque Beef Sandwich.

WELSH RAREBIT SAUCE

Milk	1 cup
Half and Half	1 cup
Flour, all purpose	¼ cup
Salt	½ teaspoon
Dry Mustard	½ teaspoon
Cayenne Pepper	To Taste
Paprika	¼ teaspoon
Oleo Margarine	¼ cup
Sharp Cheddar Cheese, shredded	2 cups
Worcestershire Sauce	1 tablespoon
YIELD:	2 cups

PREPARATION:
1. Heat milk and half and half together in a small saucepan over low heat.
2. Combine flour, salt, mustard, cayenne pepper and paprika.
3. In a medium size saucepan, melt oleo margarine and gradually add dry ingredients. Cook until mixture is smooth.
4. Combine heated milk and half and half with the oleo margarine mixture, stirring constantly until mixture is smooth and thickened. Allow to heat for 3 to 5 minutes or until the flour taste has disappeared. DO NOT ALLOW TO BOIL.

5. Reduce heat to *very low* and gradually add shredded sharp cheddar cheese, continue to stir until the cheese is well blended and the mixture is smooth.
6. Add Worcestershire sauce and stir to blend.
7. If Rarebit Sauce is not served immediately, hold sauce *hot,* covered on a double boiler set-up until time of service.

NOTE:
— Welsh Rarebit may be served over toast points or used as an entree topping when desired.

Overheating will cause sauce to thicken and oleo margarine will separate from the mixture.

MEDIUM CREAM SAUCE

Oleo Margarine	*6 tablespoons*
Flour, all purpose	*½ cup*
Milk	*4 cups*
Salt	*¾ teaspoon*
YIELD:	*1 quart*

PREPARATION:
1. Melt oleo margarine in a medium size sauce pan over low heat.
2. Blend in flour and salt.
3. Add milk *all at once.*
4. Cook quickly, stirring constantly until mixture thickens. Remove from heat.

NOTE:
— Overheating will cause sauce to thicken and oleo margarine will separate from the mixture.
— If a thinner or thicker Cream Sauce is desired, add or reduce milk accordingly.

MEDIUM CHEESE SAUCE

Oleo Margarine	*6 tablespoons*
Flour, all purpose	*½ cup*
Milk	*4 cups*
Salt	*½ teaspoon*
Sharp Cheddar Cheese, shredded	*2 cups*
YIELD:	*5 cups*

PREPARATION:
1. Melt oleo margarine in a medium size saucepan over low heat.
2. Blend in flour and salt.
3. Add milk all at once.
4. Cook quickly, stirring constantly until mixture thickens.
5. Reduce heat to very low and gradually add shredded sharp Cheddar cheese; continue to stir until the cheese is well blended and mixture is smooth.
6. If Cheese Sauce is not served immediately, hold on a double boiler set up until time of service.
7. Serve with omelettes, souffles, vegetables or as desired.

NOTE:
— Overheating will cause sauce to thicken and oleo margarine will separate from the mixture.
— If a thinner or thicker cheese sauce is desired, add or reduce milk accordingly.

MEDIUM FRICASSEE SAUCE

Oleo Margarine	*6 tablespoons*
Flour, all purpose	*½ cup*
White Pepper	*⅛ teaspoon*
Chicken Stock	*2 cups*
YIELD:	*4 cups*

PREPARATION:
1. Melt oleo margarine in a medium size sauce pan over low heat.
2. Blend in flour and white pepper.
3. Add chicken stock gradually, stirring constantly.
4. Cook quickly, stirring constantly until thickened and flour taste has disappeared.
5. Use as directed on individual recipes or as a gravy with chicken or other poultry entrees.

NOTE:
— Overheating will cause sauce to thicken and oleo margarine will separate from the mixture.
— If a thinner or thicker Fricassee Sauce is desired, add or reduce chicken stock accordingly.

ENCHILADA SAUCE (A Spicier Version of Barbeque Sauce)

Barbeque Sauce	*2 cups*
St. Louis Sauce	*2 cups*
YIELD:	*1 quart*

PREPARATION:

1. Prepare Barbeque Sauce and St. Louis Sauces as directed on individual recipes.
2. Combine Barbeque Sauce and St. Louis Sauce.
3. Heat sauces to boiling, blending thoroughly.
4. Use as directed on individual recipes for Barbeque Sauce when a spicier version is desired.

ITALIAN SAUCE

Tomatoes, canned	7 cups
Onions, ¼" dice	¼ cup
Garlic Clove, minced	½ each
Oleo Margarine	1 tablespoon
Salt	To Taste
White Pepper	To Taste
Sugar, granulated	2 teaspoons
YIELD:	4 cups

PREPARATION:
1. Drain tomatoes, reserving juice and finely dice.
2. Sauté diced onions and minced garlic in oleo margarine until tender.
3. Combine all ingredients including reserved juice from tomatoes. Bring to a boil.
4. Lower heat and simmer slowly over low heat until thickened, approximately 45 minutes; stir occasionally to prevent sauce from sticking.
5. If sauce is not served immediately, hold on a double boiler set up until time of service.

MEATLESS SPAGHETTI SAUCE

Onion, ⅛" dice	1 cup
Garlic Clove, minced	½ each
Oleo Margarine	1 tablespoon
Tomatoes	2½ cups
Tomato Puree	1 cup + 2 tablespoons
Salt	To Taste
White Pepper	To Taste
Chicken Base	1 tablespoon + 1 teaspoon
Parmesan Cheese	2 tablespoons + 1 teaspoon
Sugar, granulated	3 tablespoons
Bay Leaf	1 each
Fresh Parsley, finely chopped	⅓ cup
YIELD:	Approximately 3 cups

PREPARATION:
1. Sauté onion and garlic in oleo margarine until tender but not browned.
2. Drain tomatoes, reserving juice, and finely dice.
3. Combine all ingredients including reserved juice from tomatoes. Bring to a boil.
4. Lower heat and simmer, partially covered, for 45 minutes to 1 hour depending on thickness desired. Stir occasionally to prevent sauce from sticking.

CREOLE SAUCE

Oleo Margarine	2 tablespoons
Green Peppers, ½ " dice	1¼ cups
Onions, ½ " dice	1¾ cups
Mushrooms, ½ " dice	1 cup
Tomatoes, canned (with juice) ½ " dice	3 cups
Salt	To Taste
White Pepper	To Taste
Cornstarch	2 teaspoons
Water	⅛ cup
YIELD:	4½ cups

PREPARATION:
1. Sauté the diced green peppers, onions and mushrooms in oleo margarine until vegetables are tender but not brown.
2. Add diced tomatoes, salt and white pepper; simmer slowly until well blended.
3. Dissolve cornstarch in water and gradually add to sauce, stirring constantly until thoroughly blended and sauce thickens.

SAVORY TOMATO SAUCE

Oleo Margarine	*1 tablespoon*
Garlic, crushed	*½ clove*
Green Pepper, ¼" dice	*⅛ cup*
Onions, ¼" dice	*1 cup*
Tomatoes, canned (with juice), ¼" dice	*1½ cups*
Tomato Puree	*½ cup*
Salt	*To Taste*
White Pepper	*⅛ teaspoon*
Chicken Base	*2 teaspoons*
Water, cold	*2 tablespoons*
Cornstarch	*2 teaspoons*
YIELD:	*2 cups*

PREPARATION:
1. Sauté crushed garlic, diced green peppers and onions in oleo margarine until vegetables are tender but not browned.
2. Add diced canned tomatoes with juice.
3. Add tomato puree, salt, white pepper, and chicken base. Bring to a boil.
4. Reduce heat and simmer slowly for 15 minutes, stirring frequently to prevent sticking.
5. Combine cornstarch with cold water, blending until thoroughly combined. Gradually add to tomato mixture.
6. Stirring constantly, cook approximately 5 minutes or until sauce is thickened and clear.

BARBEQUE SAUCE

Oleo Margarine	*5 tablespoons + 2 teaspoons*
Onions, ⅛" dice	*1 cup*
Vinegar, cider	*½ cup + 1 tablespoon*
Chili Sauce	*1 cup + 1 tablespoon*
Tomato Puree	*1 cup + 1 tablespoon*
Brown Sugar	*½ cup*
Garlic Clove, minced	*2 cloves (1 teaspoon)*
Worcestershire Sauce	*2 tablespoons + 1 teaspoon*
White Pepper	*1¼ teaspoons*
Horseradish, prepared	*1 tablespoon + 1 teaspoon*
Dry Mustard	*1 tablespoon*
Salt	*To Taste*
YIELD:	*4 cups*

PREPARATION:
1. Simmer onions in oleo margarine until tender.
2. Combine remaining ingredients. Bring mixture to a boil.
3. Reduce heat and simmer for 10 minutes, stirring frequently to blend well.
4. Use as directed on individual recipes.

ST. LOUIS SAUCE

Chili Powder	*4 teaspoons*
Dry Mustard	*3 teaspoons*
Cayenne Pepper	*To Taste*
Salt	*To Taste*
Flour, all purpose	*⅓ cup*
Worcestershire Sauce	*⅓ cup*
Catsup	*1 tablespoon + 1 teaspoon*
Tomato Paste	*⅓ cup*
Vinegar, cider	*⅓ cup*
Beef Broth	*3 cups*
YIELD:	*1 quart*

PREPARATION:
1. Blend all dry ingredients until thoroughly combined.
2. Mix Worcestershire sauce, catsup, tomato paste and vinegar.
3. Add dry ingredients to tomato mixture. Combine with beef broth.
4. Bring mixture to a boil.
5. Reduce heat and simmer for 5 to 10 minutes, stirring frequently to prevent sticking.
6. Use as directed on individual recipes.

SWEET AND SOUR SAUCE

Onion, finely chopped	1 cup
Oleo Margarine	1 tablespoon
Chicken Base	1 tablespoon
Catsup	1¼ cups
Brown Sugar	1 cup
Vinegar, cider	½ cup
Worcestershire Sauce	1½ teaspoons
Water, cold	1½ cups
Cornstarch	2 tablespoons
YIELD:	1 quart

PREPARATION:
1. In a medium size saucepan, sauté onion in oleo margarine until tender but not browned.
2. Add chicken base, catsup, brown sugar, vinegar, Worcestershire sauce and 1¼ cups of water. Bring to a boil.
3. Dissolve cornstarch in ¼ cup of water and add to the boiling mixture.
4. Reduce heat and simmer for 10 minutes to prevent sticking.
5. Use as directed on individual recipes.

BROWN GRAVY

Oleo Margarine	7½ tablespoons
Onions, ½" dice	1 cup
Celery, ½" dice	½ cup
Carrots, ½" dice	½ cup
Garlic	½ clove
Tomatoes, canned – drained and chopped	¼ cup
Parsley, chopped	1 tablespoon
Beef Base	2 tablespoons
Water	4½ cups
Thyme, leaf	Dash
Bay Leaf	½ each
White Pepper	To Taste
Flour, all purpose	¾ cup
Kitchen Bouquet	¾ teaspoon
YIELD:	1¼ quarts

PREPARATION:
1. Drain tomatoes and discard juice.
2. Melt 1½ tablespoons of oleo margarine in a 2 quart saucepan.
3. Add onions, celery, carrots and garlic; sauté for 5 minutes.
4. Cover; cook 10 minutes longer, stirring occasionally.
5. Add beef base and continue cooking for 5 minutes.
6. Add water, tomatoes, parsley, thyme, bay leaf and pepper. Bring to a boil.
7. Reduce heat and simmer covered for 30 minutes.
8. Strain through a fine mesh strainer. Discard cooked vegetables. Measure strained liquid and add water to bring liquid to 5 cups.
9. In a second saucepan, over low heat, melt remaining 6 tablespoons of oleo margarine.
10. Blend in flour and stir until thoroughly combined.
11. Gradually add strained broth to oleo/flour mixture, stirring constantly to prevent lumps from forming.
12. Add Kitchen Bouquet. Bring to a boil; reduce heat and simmer until gravy thickens. Stir frequently to prevent sticking.

VEGETABLE GRAVY

Brown Gravy	*1 quart*
Peas, frozen	*½ cup*
Carrots, raw — ¼ " dice	*⅓ cup*
Celery, raw — ¼ " dice	*⅓ cup*
Onion, raw — ¼ " dice	*⅓ cup*
Water	*¼ cup*

YIELD: *1¼ quarts*

PREPARATION:
1. In a small saucepan, cook carrots, celery and onions in ¼ cup of water just until tender. Drain thoroughly.
2. Do not cook peas. Rinse frozen peas under hot tap water to thaw.
3. Add all vegetables to hot gravy. Stir to blend.
4. Serve as desired or as directed on individual recipes.

ONION GRAVY

Brown Gravy, heated	*2 cups*
Onion, ¼" dice	*1 cup*
Oleo Margarine	*1 tablespoon*
YIELD:	*2½ cups*

PREPARATION:
1. Prepare Brown Gravy according to directions on Brown Gravy recipe.
2. Sauté diced onions in oleo margarine until tender, but not browned.
3. Combine sautéed onion mixture and heated Brown Gravy.
4. Serve as desired.

Peppercream Dressing on a Tossed Salad

SALADS, SALAD DRESSINGS

Bill Marriott's brother Paul traveled extensively, and developed a taste for dishes not commonly found in America during the Thirties and Forties. He was responsible for the Hot Shoppes serving Onion Soup Au Gratin, for example, and he was the force behind our successful Blue Cheese Dressing. Although good fortune, a good chef, and a little boy's Bar Mitzvah also played a role.

When Paul asked the "Experimental Chef" at the Hot Shoppes Commissary to develop an especially creamy Blue Cheese Dressing, he had just finished catering a Bar Mitzvah with all dairy dishes. So he had an ample supply of sour cream on hand, and remembering a slogan about necessity and invention, he plunged ahead. By the time he had exhausted his supply of sour cream, luckily enough, he had also hit upon the texture and taste that satisfied Paul. It's the same recipe we use today.

You may find it surprising that we have two "Slaws" in this section, although you wouldn't if you had ever used the wrong slaw on a sandwich. Barbeque Slaw is spicier, to complement the flavor of the meats it goes with. The other Cole Slaw is a sweeter, creamier side-dish. At Hot Shoppes, however, both have always shared two qualities: crispness, because they're made fresh daily, and what we might call firmness. Slaws shouldn't be wet, or they'll soak through the sandwiches they're sometimes used with. To see if you've mixed the dressing and the cabbage in proper proportions, perform the Bill Marriott Cole Slaw test; invert a dish of slaw on a plate. If a puddle forms around the slaw in the second plate, you're not quite ready for the Hot Shoppes kitchen.

CHICKEN SALAD

Mayonnaise	1 cup
Lemon Juice, fresh	1 tablespoon
Salt	To Taste
White Pepper	To Taste
Chicken, cooked, skinned and deboned — ¼" to ½" dice	3 cups
Celery, ¼" dice	2 cups
YIELD:	3¾ cups

PREPARATION:
1. Combine mayonnaise with lemon juice, salt and white pepper. Stir to blend well.
2. Add diced chicken and celery and stir until all ingredients are evenly distributed.
3. Cover and refrigerate until time of service.
4. Serve as desired for salads or sandwiches.

TUNA SALAD

Mayonnaise	⅞ cup
Lemon Juice, fresh	2½ teaspoons
Salt	To Taste
White Pepper	⅛ teaspoon
Tuna Fish, drained	2 cups
Celery, ¼" dice	2 cups
YIELD:	Approximately 5 cups

PREPARATION:
1. Combine mayonnaise with lemon juice, salt and white pepper. Stir to blend well.
2. Add diced celery and drained tuna fish, which has been broken into 1" flakes. Stir just enough to combine. Do not break up tuna any smaller than 1" flakes.
3. Cover and refrigerate until time of service.
4. Serve as desired for salads or sandwiches.

DEVILED EGG SALAD

Mayonnaise	¼ cup
Mustard, prepared	1 teaspoon
Onion, minced	½ teaspoon
Pickle, kosher dill — ⅛" dice	⅓ cup
Salt	To Taste
White Pepper	¼ teaspoon
Celery, ⅛" dice	½ cup
Eggs, hard cooked — ¼" dice	7 each
YIELD:	2¼ cups

PREPARATION:
1. Combine mayonnaise with prepared mustard, minced onion, chopped dill pickle, salt and white pepper. Stir to blend well.
2. Add diced celery and eggs. Stir just enough to combine.
3. Cover and refrigerate until time of service.
4. Serve as desired for salads or sandwiches.

BARBEQUE SLAW

Vinegar, cider	2 tablespoons
Sugar, granulated	1 teaspoon
Celery Seed	1 teaspoon
Pickle, kosher dill — ¼" dice	⅓ cup
Mustard, prepared	1 teaspoon
Mustard Seed	2 teaspoons
Cabbage, chopped — ⅛"	2 cups
YIELD:	2 cups

PREPARATION:
1. Combine vinegar, sugar, mustard seed and celery seed. Bring to a boil.
2. Reduce heat and simmer for 2 minutes. Add diced pickle and return mixture to a boil.
3. Remove from heat. Add prepared mustard and refrigerate until thoroughly chilled.
4. Pour chilled pickle mixture over chopped cabbage. Toss to thoroughly combine all ingredients.
5. Refrigerate until time of service.
6. Serve with Barbeque Sandwiches as directed.

COLE SLAW

Green Cabbage, shredded	*4½ cups*
Carrots, shredded	*⅓ cup*
Onions, ⅛" dice	*1½ tablespoons*
Cole Slaw Dressing	*1 cup*
YIELD:	*6 to 8 servings*

PREPARATION:
1. Mix cabbage, carrots and onions thoroughly to evenly distribute all ingredients.
2. Toss with Cole Slaw Dressing.
3. Cover and refrigerate until time of service.

MARINATED TOMATO AND GREEN PEPPER SALAD

Tomatoes, fresh — medium size	*4 each*
Green Pepper Rings — ¼" cut	*8 each*
Tomato Marinade	
Water	*½ cup*
Vinegar, cider	*¼ cup*
Salt	*¼ teaspoon*
Sugar, granulated	*1 tablespoon*
Salad Oil	*¼ cup*
YIELD:	*6 to 8 servings*

PREPARATION:
1. Cut tomatoes in half lengthwise. Remove core and cut each tomato half into three wedges.
2. Cut green pepper rings in half.
3. Mix tomatoes and green peppers together.
4. Combine all Tomato Marinade ingredients in a small mixing bowl. Beat with a wire whip until well blended.
5. Pour Tomato Marinade over tomatoes and green peppers.

Cover and refrigerate until time of service. Allow to marinate for two hours or overnight

TOMATO ASPIC

Tomato Juice	2¾ cups
Salt	1 teaspoon
Sugar, granulated	1 tablespoon
Onion, finely chopped	⅓ cup
Celery, ¼" dice	1 cup
Plain Gelatin	2 tablespoons + 1 teaspoon
Water, cold	⅓ cup
Lemon Juice, fresh	1 tablespoon + 1 teaspoon
Horseradish, prepared	1 tablespoon
Stuffed Olives, chopped	1½ tablespoons

YIELD: 6 to 8 servings

PREPARATION:
1. Add salt, sugar, chopped onion and ¼ cup of chopped celery to tomato juice. Bring to a boil.
2. Reduce heat and simmer for 5 minutes.
3. Soften gelatin in cold water. Add hot tomato juice mixture to gelatin and stir until gelatin is completely dissolved.
4. Add lemon juice and horseradish.
5. Chill mixture for approximately 40 minutes until partially set.
6. Add remaining ¾ cup of chopped celery and the olives.
7. Pour into 3 to 4 ounce individual molds. Refrigerate until firm.

NOTE:
— To unmold Tomato Aspic: Dip each mold to rim in warm water for a few seconds. Loosen edges with a spatula. Pick up mold and tilt it. Carefully ease aspic away from one side of the mold to let air in, then rotate mold to loosen on all sides. Place serving plate over mold, then invert and lift mold straight up.

COTTAGE CHEESE AND TOMATO SALAD

Tomato Juice	*2 cups*
Vinegar, cider	*2½ teaspoons*
Lemon Gelatin	*1 – 3 oz. package*
French Dressing	*¼ cup*
Cottage Cheese	*1 pound*
Green Pepper, finely chopped	*1 tablespoon + 1 teaspoon*
Cabbage, finely chopped	*1 cup*
Mayonnaise	*3 tablespoons*
Onion, finely chopped	*2 teaspoons*
YIELD:	*6 to 8 servings*

PREPARATION:
1. Heat tomato juice and vinegar.
2. Add heated juice to the lemon gelatin. Stir until gelatin is completely dissolved.
3. Place approximately 2 tablespoons of gelatin mixture in each of 3 to 4 ounce individual molds and place in refrigerator to set.
4. Add mayonnaise and French dressing to cottage cheese and mix well.
5. Add the remainder of the tomato juice/gelatin solution to the cottage cheese.
6. Add the finely chopped green pepper and cabbage.
7. Divide mixture evenly into 3 or 4 ounce individual molds, placing mixture on top of the jellied tomato mixture.
8. Refrigerate until firm.

NOTE:
— To Unmold Gelatin Salad: Dip each mold to rim in warm water for a few seconds. Loosen edges with a spatula. Pick up mold and tilt it. Carefully ease gelatin away from one side of the mold to let air in, then rotate mold to loosen on all sides. Place serving plate over mold, then invert and lift mold straight up.

HOT POTATO SALAD

Water, cold	6 cups
Salt	1½ teaspoons
Potatoes, fresh — medium size, peeled	6 to 7 each
Bacon	6 slices

Potato Salad Dressing:

Bacon Fat	5 tablespoons
Onion, ¼" dice	¾ cup
Flour, all purpose	1 tablespoon
Vinegar, cider	½ cup + 1 tablespoon
Water	½ cup + 2 tablespoons
Dry Mustard	⅛ teaspoon
Sugar, granulated	1 tablespoon + 1 teaspoon
Salt	½ teaspoon
Poultry Seasoning	¼ teaspoon
White Pepper	¼ teaspoon
YIELD:	6 to 8 servings

PREPARATION:
1. Bring water and salt to boiling in a heavy saucepan.
2. Add potatoes. Cover and cook until potatoes are *almost* done, about 15 to 20 minutes. DO NOT OVERCOOK.
3. Drain well.
4. Cook bacon until crisp; drain and coarsely crumble. Reserve bacon fat for Potato Salad Dressing.
5. TO MAKE POTATO SALAD DRESSING:
   - Sauté diced onion in measured amount of bacon fat.
   - Add flour to fat and blend well.
   - Heat vinegar, water, dry mustard, salt, poultry seasoning and white pepper; add to flour and fat mixture stirring constantly until thickened.
   - Keep sauce hot until needed.
6. Slice drained potatoes into ¼" thick crosswise slices.
7. Place one half of potatoes in a greased 2 quart glass baking dish or casserole. Sprinkle with half of bacon crumbles and half of dressing.
8. Top with remaining potatoes, then crumbled bacon and dressing.
9. Cover and bake in a preheated 350°F oven until heated thoroughly and most of sauce is absorbed, approximately 20 to 30 minutes.

PICKLED BEET SALAD

Beets, sliced	1 – 16 oz. can
Vinegar, cider	3 tablespoons + 2 teaspoons
Sugar, granulated	2 tablespoons
Bay Leaf	½ each
Onion, sliced – ¼ " thick	¾ cup
Celery, sliced – ⅛ " thick	¾ cup
YIELD:	6 to 8 servings

PREPARATION:
1. Drain beets, reserving juice.
2. Combine beet juice, vinegar, sugar and bay leaf in a small saucepan. Bring to a boil.
3. Combine drained sliced beets, onions and celery. Add hot juice mixture.
4. Cover and refrigerate until time of service. Allow to marinate at least 30 minutes before serving to allow flavors to blend.
5. Serve as desired.
6. Garnish with parsley or watercress.

EGG AND ASPARAGUS SALAD

Lettuce, iceberg or leaf	To Line Plate
Egg, hard cooked	1 each
Asparagus Tips	2 each
Pimiento Strip	1 each
YIELD:	1 serving

PREPARATION:
1. Line plate with crisp lettuce.
2. Slice egg and fan out 1 sliced egg on one side of plate.
3. Place 2 asparagus tips next to egg.
4. Garnish asparagus with a thin strip of pimiento across center of asparagus.
5. Garnish plate with parsley or watercress.

APPLE WALDORF SALAD

Lemon Juice	1 tablespoon + 1 teaspoon
Mayonnaise	½ cup
Salt	¾ teaspoon
Apples, washed and cored	3½ cups
Celery, ½ " dice	1½ cups
YIELD:	6 to 8 servings

PREPARATION:
1. Mix the lemon juice with mayonnaise and salt and blend well.
2. Dice washed apples into ½ " to 1 " pieces and add to mayonnaise mixture. Stir apples to cover completely with mayonnaise and to prevent darkening.
3. Add celery and stir to blend.
4. Cover and refrigerate until time of service.

NOTE:
— If celery is very moist, it will break down mayonnaise.
— If desired, ½ to 1 cup of seedless raisins and/or coarsely chopped walnuts may be added to the salad for variation.

If apple skins are tough or poor in color, peel apples.

TROPICAL FRESH FRUIT PLATTER

Melon Wedge (Cantaloupe, Honeydew or Watermelon)	1 medium size wedge
Grapes — white, red or black	1 cluster
Fresh Pineapple — ¼ " thick wedges	4 wedges
Fresh Apple, Red Delicious — 1/16" thick wedges	4 wedges
Lemon Juice, fresh	As Needed
Fresh Grapefruit Sections	3 each
Strawberries	4 each
Lettuce Cups	4 each
Lettuce, shredded	¼ cup
Cottage Cheese or Sherbet	¼ cup or 1 medium size scoop
Parsley Sprig, large	1 each
YIELD:	1 serving

PREPARATION:
1. Wash melon and cut in half; remove seeds. Peel and cut into medium size wedges.
2. Wash grapes by placing bunches in a large bowl of water. Drain thoroughly and cut in clusters.
3. Wash pineapple. Cut a ¼" thick slice from bottom and top of pineapple. Cut pineapple lengthwise into quarters. Remove core from each quarter. Cut through peel into ¼" thick slices.
4. Wash, core and cut apple into 16 wedges. Do not peel. Dip in lemon juice to prevent apple from turning brown.
5. Wash, peel, section and seed grapefruit.
6. Wash strawberries. Drain thoroughly. Do not remove stems.
7. Place all portioned fruit in a pan or on a platter. Cover and refrigerate until time of service.

SERVICE:
1. Arrange 4 pineapple wedges in a lettuce cup. Place at one end of platter.
2. Alternate 4 apple wedges (red skin facing upward) with 3 grapefruit sections in a lettuce cup. Place at other end of platter.
3. Place a melon wedge and a cluster of grapes in a lettuce cup. Place at center back of platter.
4. Line a lettuce cup with a ¼ cup of shredded lettuce. At time of service, top with listed cottage cheese or sherbet. Place toward front edge of platter.
5. Garnish platter with 4 uncapped fresh strawberries and a large sprig of parsley.

MOLDED FRUIT SALAD

Plain Gelatin	*½ teaspoon*
Cold Water	*½ cup*
Flavored Gelatin	*1 – 3 oz. package*
Boiling Water or Fruit Juice	*¾ cup*
Ice Cubes	*1½ cups*
Pineapple, canned and drained – ½" dice	*½ cup*
Peaches, canned and drained – ½" dice	*⅓ cup*
Apples, peeled and cored – ½" dice	*⅔ cup*
Oranges, peeled, seeded and drained – ½" dice	*⅓ cup*
YIELD:	*6 to 8 servings*

PREPARATION:
1. Soften plain gelatin in cold water.
2. Add boiling water to flavored gelatin and combine with softened gelatin. Stir until gelatins are completely dissolved.
3. Add ice; stir continuously until all ice is melted completely.
4. Add drained fruits and apples to gelatin mixture as soon as it begins to thicken. Blend to distribute fruit evenly.
5. Divide mixture evenly into 3 or 4 ounce individual molds.
6. Refrigerate until firm.
7. Serve as desired as a salad or as a dessert garnished with whipped cream.

NOTE:
— Any flavored gelatin may be used with this recipe: cherry, strawberry, raspberry, lime, etc.
— To Unmold Gelatin Salad: Dip each mold to rim in warm water for a few seconds. Loosen edges with a spatula. Pick up mold and tilt it. Carefully ease gelatin away from one side of the mold to let air in, then rotate mold to loosen on all sides. Place serving plate over mold, then invert and lift mold straight up.

Do not use fresh pineapple, it prevents the gelatin from congealing.

PINEAPPLE CHEESE SALAD

Plain Gelatin	½ teaspoon
Water, cold	2 tablespoons
Water, boiling	½ cup
Lemon Gelatin	1 – 3 oz. package
Pineapple Juice	6 tablespoons
Ice Cubes	1½ cups
Mayonnaise	¼ cup
Sharp Cheddar Cheese, shredded	½ cup
Maraschino Cherries — cut in half lengthwise and drained	8 each
Pineapple, canned and drained — ½ " dice	½ cup
Cream	½ cup
YIELD:	6 to 8 servings

PREPARATION:
1. Soften plain gelatin in cold water.
2. Combine softened gelatin with lemon gelatin and add to boiling water. Stir until gelatins are completely dissolved.
3. Add pineapple juice and ice. Stir continuously until all ice is melted. Refrigerate until partially set.
4. Combine shredded sharp Cheddar cheese with pineapple and mayonnaise. Blend until smooth.
5. Add cream to the pineapple/cheese mixture. Blend until smooth.
6. When the gelatin begins to thicken and is partially set, add the pineapple/cheese mixture and maraschino cherry halves. (Be sure to drain cherries thoroughly on paper towels before adding to the mixture.)
7. Distribute mixture evenly into 3 or 4 ounce individual molds.
8. Refrigerate until firm.

NOTE:
— Do not use fresh pineapple. It prevents the gelatin from congealing.
— To unmold gelatin salad: Dip each mold to rim in warm water for a few seconds. Loosen edges with a spatula. Pick up mold and tilt it. Carefully ease gelatin away from one side of the mold to let air in, then rotate mold to loosen on all sides. Place serving plate over mold, then invert and lift straight up.

BANANA PECAN SALAD

Plain Gelatin	*½ teaspoon*
Cold Water	*½ cup*
Flavored Gelatin	*1 — 3 oz. package*
Boiling Water or Fruit Juice	*¾ cup*
Ice Cubes	*1½ cups*
Pecans, coarsely chopped	*⅔ cup*
Bananas — peeled and sliced ¼"	*2 each*
YIELD:	*6 to 8 servings*

PREPARATION:
1. Soften plain gelatin in cold water.
2. Add boiling water or fruit juice to flavored gelatin and combine with softened gelatin. Stir until gelatins are completely dissolved.
3. Add ice; stir continuously until all ice is melted completely.
4. Add pecan pieces and bananas to gelatin mixture as soon as it begins to thicken. Blend to distribute fruit evenly.

5. Divide mixture evenly into 3 or 4 ounce individual molds.
6. Refrigerate until firm.
7. Serve as desired as a salad or as a dessert garnished with whipped cream.

NOTE:
— Any flavored gelatin may be used with this recipe.
— To Unmold Gelatin Salad: Dip each mold to rim in warm water for a few seconds. Loosen edges with a spatula. Pick up mold and tilt it. Carefully ease gelatin away from one side of the mold to let air in, then rotate mold to loosen on all sides. Place serving plate over mold, then invert and lift mold straight up.

CELERY, APPLE AND NUT SALAD

Plain Gelatin	½ *teaspoon*
Cold Water	¼ *cup*
Lemon Gelatin	1— 3 oz. package
Boiling Water	¾ *cup*
Vinegar	1 tablespoon + 2 teaspoons
Salt	Dash
Pecans, coarsely chopped	¼ *cup*
Apples, unpeeled and cored— ½ " dice	½ *cup*
Celery, ¼ " *dice*	½ *cup*
Ice Cubes	1½ *cups*
YIELD:	*6 to 8 servings*

PREPARATION:
1. Soften plain gelatin in cold water.
2. Add boiling water to flavored gelatin and salt; combine with softened gelatin. Stir until gelatins are completely dissolved.
3. Add vinegar.
4. Add ice; stir continuously until all ice is melted completely.
5. Fold pecans, apples, and celery into mixture.
6. Divide mixture evenly into 3 or 4 ounce individual molds.
7. Refrigerate until firm.

NOTE:
— To unmold Gelatin Salad: Dip each mold to rim in warm water for a few seconds. Loosen edges with a spatula. Pick up mold and tilt it. Carefully ease gelatin away from one side of the mold to let air in, then rotate mold to loosen on all sides. Place serving plate over mold, then invert and lift mold straight up.

HEAVENLY HASH

Mandarin Oranges	2 cups
Pineapple Tidbits	2 cups
Coconut, flaked	2 cups
Marshmallows, miniature	2 cups
Sour Cream	1¾ cups
YIELD:	6 to 8 servings

PREPARATION:
1. Drain mandarin oranges and pineapple tidbits.
2. Combine with coconut, marshmallows and sour cream.
3. Cover and refrigerate until time of service.
4. Garnish as desired or with maraschino cherries and additional mandarin oranges.

PEARADISE SALAD

Lettuce, iceberg or leaf	To Line Bowl
Cottage Cheese	½ cup
Pear Halves, cut in half lengthwise	4 quarters
Strawberries, fresh	5 each
YIELD:	1 serving

PREPARATION:
1. Line serving plate or bowl with iceberg or leaf lettuce.
2. Place cottage cheese in center of lettuce.
3. Stand pear quarters close to cottage cheese with points toward top.
4. Place fresh strawberries between points of fruit and one on top of cottage cheese.
5. Garnish with parsley or watercress.
6. Serve with saltine crackers or roll and butter.

PEPPERCREAM DRESSING

Eggs, large	4 each
Salad Oil	2 cups
Worcestershire Sauce	1 teaspoon
Tabasco Sauce	¼ teaspoon
Onion Juice	1 tablespoon + ½ teaspoon
Lemon Juice	½ cup
Vinegar, cider	2 teaspoons
Peppercorns, crushed	1 tablespoon
Parmesan Cheese	1 cup
Dry Mustard	1 teaspoon
Garlic Powder	½ teaspoon
Salt	1 teaspoon
YIELD:	1 quart

PREPARATION:
1. Beat eggs with a rotary or electric mixer until well mixed, but not light.
2. Add oil in a very slow thread-like stream while continuing to beat.
3. When oil is completely blended, add remaining ingredients. Continue beating until well blended.
4. Cover and refrigerate until time of service.
5. Stir dressing well before service.

Note: Use within three days of preparation.

CLEAR FRENCH DRESSING

Sugar, granulated	½ cup + 3 tablespoons
Paprika	1¼ teaspoons
Salt	¾ teaspoon
Celery Seed	1½ teaspoons
Dry Mustard	1½ tablespoons
White Pepper	½ teaspoon
Vinegar	1 cup
Lemon Juice, fresh	¼ cup
Onion Juice, fresh	6 tablespoons
Worcestershire Sauce	1¾ tablespoons
Salad Oil	2 cups
YIELD:	3½ cups

PREPARATION:
1. Mix all dry ingredients together to thoroughly combine.
2. Combine vinegar, fresh lemon and onion juices and Worcestershire sauce.
3. Add dry ingredients and mix well.
4. Add oil to the mixture and continue mixing until sugar is dissolved and all ingredients are well blended.
5. Cover and refrigerate until time of service.

Note: This dressings is best when made one day ahead. It mellows as it stands.

BLUE CHEESE DRESSING

White Pepper	¼ teaspoon
Vinegar, cider	1 tablespoon + 1 teaspoon
Sour Cream	1⅔ cup
Mayonnaise	1⅔ cup
Blue Cheese	1½ cups
YIELD:	1 quart

PREPARATION:
1. Add white pepper, vinegar and sour cream to mayonnaise.
2. Break up blue cheese in small crumbles and add to mayonnaise mixture. Stir gently until thoroughly combined.
3. Cover and refrigerate until time of service.

NOTE:
— Allow several hours for flavor to mellow before serving.

YOGURT DRESSING (For Vegetable Salads)

Yogurt, plain	2 cups
Mayonnaise	½ cup
Lemon Juice, fresh	2 tablespoons
Onion, finely grated	1 tablespoon + 1¼ teaspoons
Salt	½ teaspoon
Sugar, granulated	1 teaspoon
White Pepper	¼ teaspoon
YIELD:	2½ cups

PREPARATION:
1. Grate onion as finely as possible. Use grated pulp and juice when making dressing.
2. Combine all ingredients and mix thoroughly, stirring until well blended.
3. Cover and refrigerate until time of service.
4. Serve as a dressing for vegetable salads.

HONEY YOGURT DRESSING (For Fruit Salads)

Yogurt, plain	*1 cup*
Honey	*3 tablespoons*
Lemon Peel, fresh — grated	*¼ teaspoon*
YIELD:	*Approximately 1¼ cups*

PREPARATION:
1. Wash, dry lemon and finely grate peel.
2. Combine all ingredients and mix thoroughly, stirring until well blended.
3. Cover and refrigerate until time of service.
4. Serve as a dressing for fruit salads.

PINEAPPLE MAYONNAISE

Mayonnaise	*2 cups*
Pineapple Sundae Topping	*½ cup*
YIELD:	*2½ cups*

PREPARATION:
1. Combine mayonnaise and pineapple sundae topping and mix thoroughly, stirring until well blended.
2. Cover and refrigerate until time of service.
3. Use as a salad dressing or a dip for fresh fruits.

COLE SLAW DRESSING

Sugar, granulated	⅓ cup + 1 tablespoon
Salt	1 teaspoon
White Pepper	¾ teaspoon
Celery Seed	1¾ teaspoon
Horseradish	2 tablespoons
Mustard, prepared	1 tablespoon + 1 teaspoon
Mayonnaise	3 cups
Vinegar, cider	⅓ cup + 1½ teaspoons
Half and Half	⅓ cup + 1½ teaspoons

YIELD: 1 quart

PREPARATION:
1. Combine sugar, salt, pepper and celery seed.
2. Add horseradish and prepared mustard.
3. Add to mayonnaise and stir to blend well.
4. Add vinegar, stirring to blend thoroughly; then add half and half last and continue blending until all ingredients are combined.
5. Cover and refrigerate until time of service.
6. Serve as directed as a dressing on Cole Slaw.

Mighty Mo

SANDWICHES

We'll begin with a potentially disappointing piece of news—Hot Shoppes Regulars will be hard pressed to find the Barbeque Sandwich rolls they've come to expect. This might not bother those who've never had a Hot Shoppes barbeque sandwich, but anyone who remembers those rectangular, sweet, slightly dense rolls, steam heated and piled high with barbeque pork, will likely be upset to discover those rolls are no longer available. So we recommend you use a plain hamburger roll, or perhaps, another slightly denser bun.

Rolls notwithstanding, you cannot cut corners on the Barbeque Beef, Pork, and Chicken. We recommend you prepare the sauces and the meats one day before you serve them, and let them sit overnight in your refrigerator. That's what the Hot Shoppes have always done, and the result is a more even blend of spices.

The Mighty Mo has also been a Hot Shoppes classic through the years. Because it was the first triple-decker hamburger in the Washington area, however, no one knew what to call it—so one of Mr. Marriott's principal assistants organized a contest (he also directed a contest to name the "Teen Twist" sandwich). The winner chose the nickname of the great battleship Missouri, perhaps because she knew our big juicy sandwich would make a considerable splash with hamburger fans. And these burgers became so well known, that when a Washington radio station donated a white tiger named Mohemi to the National Zoo, he was nicknamed "Mighty Mo" (in the years that followed, Bill Marriott and the tiger developed a cautiously warm relationship, often posing together for publicity photographs).

MIGHTY MO

Sesame Seed Hamburger Roll, uncut	*1 each*
Oleo Margarine, softened	*1 tablespoon*
Hamburger Patties, ⅛ lb. (2 ounces)	*2 each*
Salt	*To Taste*
White Pepper	*To Taste*
Lettuce, shredded	*1 tablespoon*
American Cheese	*1 slice*
Mighty Mo Sauce	*4 teaspoons*
Dill Pickle Chips	*2 each*
YIELD:	*1 serving*

PREPARATION:
1. Prepare Mighty Mo Sauce according to instructions given on recipe.
2. Cut sesame seed hamburger roll crosswise into three equal slices.
3. Spread bottom, top and one side of center cut of bun with softened oleo margarine.
4. Grill bun until lightly browned and heated throughout.
5. Shape hamburger into thin 4″ diameter patties.
6. Grill hamburger very lightly on both sides. DO NOT OVERCOOK.
7. Grill second hamburger very lightly on one side, turn and top with one slice of American cheese and grill lightly. Do not overcook.
8. Spread 2 teaspoons of Mighty Mo Sauce on bottom of roll.
9. Top dressing with shredded lettuce, then hamburger.
10. Top hamburger with middle layer of bun, grilled side up and spread with remaining 2 teaspoons of Mighty Mo Sauce.
11. Top with cheeseburger.
12. Place 2 dill pickle chips on cheese. Cover pickle with top of bun. Do not cut.

NOTE:
— If uncut sesame seed hamburger rolls are not available in your local grocery, the bottom half of a hamburger roll may be substituted for the center section.

TEEN TWIST

Ham, thinly sliced	*4 oz. or As Desired*
American Cheese – cut in half lengthwise	*1 slice*
Tomato Slice	*2 each*
Lettuce, shredded	*As Needed*
Tartar Sauce	*1 tablespoon*
Oleo Margarine, softened	*As Needed*
Twist Roll, sliced lengthwise	*1 each*
YIELD:	*1 serving*

Teen twist

PREPARATION:

1. Spread both sides of sliced roll with softened oleo margarine.
2. Place the two halves of American cheese on bottom half of roll, covering as much of roll as possible.
3. Separate thinly sliced ham and place on top of cheese, covering as much of the cheese as possible and fluffing to build full volume.
4. Place sandwich on grill with ham touching the surface of a grill or frying pan. Place top half of roll on grill.
5. Heat until ham is hot.
6. Remove from heat and top ham with 2 slices of tomato. Cover with shredded lettuce.
7. Spread 1 tablespoon of tartar sauce on the top half of the grilled roll and place on top of the sandwich.
8. Cut in half diagonally and serve as desired.

BARBEQUE BEEF

Beef, cooked well done — ⅛" dice or sliced	*4 cups*
Barbeque Sauce	*1⅓ cups*
St. Louis Sauce	*1⅓ cups*
Barbeque Slaw	*As Needed*
YIELD:	*8 to 10 servings*

PREPARATION:
1. Prepare Barbeque and St. Louis Sauces and Barbeque Slaw according to instructions given on individual recipes.
2. Trim beef free from all fat and dice into ⅛″ pieces.
3. Combine 1⅓ cups of Barbeque Sauce and 1⅓ cups of St. Louis Sauce with diced beef. Simmer slowly until meat is very tender and has absorbed most of the sauce.
4. Hold heated until time of service. Keep covered to prevent excess evaporation of barbeque sauce.
5. Place barbeque slaw on the bottom half of a grilled or toasted sandwich roll.
6. Top with beef barbeque, spreading to the edges of the roll.
7. Place top half of the roll on barbeque.

NOTE:
— Serve with Hot Sauce, if desired.
— Many variations of Barbeque Beef have been developed over the years. This recipe reflects one of the most popular.

Barbeque flavor is best when barbeque is prepared one day in advance of service to allow ingredients to marinate and flavors to blend.

BARBEQUE PORK

Pork, cooked well done — ⅛″ dice or sliced	3 cups
St. Louis Sauce	2 cups
Barbeque Sauce	⅔ cup
Barbeque Slaw	As Needed

YIELD:	6 to 8 servings

PREPARATION:
1. Prepare Barbeque and St. Louis Sauces and Barbeque Slaw according to instructions given on individual recipes.
2. Trim pork free from all fat and dice into ⅛″ pieces.
3. Combine ⅔ cup of Barbeque Sauce and 2 cups of St. Louis Sauce with diced pork. Simmer slowly until meat is very tender and has absorbed most of the sauce.
4. Hold heated until time of service. Keep covered to prevent excess evaporation of barbeque sauce.
5. Place barbeque slaw on the bottom half of a grilled or toasted sandwich roll.
6. Top with pork barbeque, spreading to the edges of the roll.

7. Place top half of the roll on barbeque.

NOTE:
— Barbeque flavor is best when barbeque is prepared one day in advance of service to allow ingredients to marinate and flavors to blend.
— Serve with Hot Sauce, if desired.
— Many variations of Barbeque Pork have been developed over the years. This recipe reflects one of the most popular.

BARBEQUE CHICKEN

Chicken, cooked, skinned and deboned — ½" to 1" dice	*4½ cups*
St. Louis Sauce	*1⅓ cups*
Medium Fricassee Sauce	*1⅓ cups*
Beef Broth	*⅔ cup*
Barbeque Slaw	*As Needed*
YIELD:	*8 to 10 servings*

PREPARATION:
1. Prepare St. Louis and Medium Fricassee Sauces and Barbeque Slaw according to instructions given on individual recipes.
2. Combine 1⅓ cups of St. Louis and 1⅓ cups of Medium Fricassee Sauces with ⅔ cup of beef broth and bring to a simmer.
3. Add the diced cooked chicken and continue simmering until meat has absorbed most of the sauce.
4. Hold heated until time of service. Keep covered to prevent excess evaporation of barbeque sauce.
5. Place barbeque slaw on the bottom half of a grilled or toasted sandwich roll.
6. Top with chicken barbeque, spreading to the edges of the roll.
7. Place top half of the roll on barbeque.

NOTE:
— Serve with Hot Sauce, if desired.
— Many variations of Barbeque Chicken have been developed over the years. This recipe reflects one of the most popular.

THE BUCKBOARD

Ham, thinly sliced	*Approximately 1½ oz. or As Desired*
Swiss Cheese, thinly sliced	*1 slice*
Russian Dressing	*2 tablespoons*
Rye Bread	*2 slices*
Oleo Margarine, softened	*As Needed*
Cole Slaw	*⅓ cup*
Lettuce Cup, large	*1 each*
Tomato Slice	*2 each*
YIELD:	*1 serving*

PREPARATION:
1. Spread 1 slice of rye bread with softened oleo margarine.
2. Place thinly sliced Swiss cheese on rye bread.
3. Top Swiss cheese with cole slaw, spreading evenly to cover entire slice of bread.
4. Place 1½ ounce of thinly sliced ham on top of cole slaw, arranging evenly to cover bread.
5. Spread 1½ tablespoons of Russian dressing on second slice of rye bread, spreading evenly to edges.
6. Place second slice of bread on top of sliced ham, with Russian dressing, with dressing touching ham.
7. Cut sandwich in thirds and arrange in a fan shape on serving plate.

HAMBURGER ROYALE

Hamburger, ¼ lb.	*1 each*
Salt	*To Taste*
White Pepper	*To Taste*
Tomato Slices	*2 each*
Russian Dressing	*1 tablespoon + 1 teaspoon*
Lettuce Cup, small	*1 each*
Hamburger Roll	*1 each*
Oleo Margarine, softened	*As Needed*
YIELD:	*1 serving*

PREPARATION:
1. Spread hamburger roll with softened oleo and grill until golden brown.
2. Grill hamburger and season with salt and white pepper to taste.
3. Place grilled hamburger on bottom half of roll.
4. Place the small lettuce cup and 2 slices of tomato on other half of roll.

5. Place Russian dressing on top of hamburger.
6. Serve open faced.

NOTE:
— Mighty Mo Sauce or Celery Sauce may be substituted for Russian dressing, if desired.

THE TALK OF THE TOWN

Barbeque Sauce, heated	*2 tablespoons*
Hamburger Patty, approximately ¼ lb. — cooked	*1 each*
Sharp Cheddar Cheese, shredded	*⅓ cup*
Lettuce Cup	*1 each*
Tomato Slices	*2 each*
Parsley Sprig	*1 each*
English Muffin	*1 each*
Butter, softened	*As Needed*
YIELD:	*1 serving*

PREPARATION:
1. Split and toast English muffin. Butter each half and place in center of serving plate.
2. Overlap cooked hamburger on both English muffin halves.
3. Pour 2 tablespoons of heated barbeque sauce over meat and muffin, in a stream line, not covering the meat entirely.
4. Top sauce with ⅓ cup of shredded sharp Cheddar cheese.
5. Garnish serving plate with 2 tomato slices placed in the lettuce cup and a parsley sprig.

CRAB CAKE SANDWICH

Crab Cake	*1 each*
Hamburger Roll	*1 each*
Oleo Margarine, softened	*As Needed*
Tartar Sauce	*1 tablespoon*
Cole Slaw	*¼ cup*
Parsley Sprig	*1 each*
YIELD:	*1 serving*

PREPARATION:
1. Prepare crab cake mixture according to instructions on Crab Cake recipe.
2. Shape crab cake mixture flat to a 3″ diameter before breading. Bread as instructed.
3. Deep fry breaded crab cake in a preheated 350° F deep fryer or electric skillet until golden brown, approximately 3 to 3½ minutes. Drain on a wire rack or paper towel.
4. Spread hamburger roll with softened oleo margarine and grill until golden brown.
5. Place grilled roll open face on serving plate.
6. Spread bottom half of grilled roll with 1 tablespoon tartar sauce. Top sauce with crab cake.
7. Place parsley sprig on top half of roll.
8. Garnish serving plate with cole slaw.

GRILLED REUBEN

Rye Bread	2 slices
Oleo Margarine	As Needed
Russian Dressing	2 tablespoons
Swiss Cheese, thinly sliced	3 slices
Corned Beef, thinly sliced	1½ ounces
Sauerkraut, drained thoroughly	¼ cup
Pickle Wedge	1 each
YIELD:	1 serving

PREPARATION:
1. Spread one side of rye bread with softened oleo margarine.
2. Spread the other side with 1 tablespoon of Russian dressing.
3. Place Swiss cheese on top of dressing.
4. Top cheese with thoroughly drained sauerkraut.
5. Arrange corned beef over sauerkraut to cover to edges of bread.
6. Spread second slice of rye bread with softened oleo margarine on one side and 1 tablespoon of Russian dressing on the other side.
7. Close sandwich with oleo side facing up.
8. Place sandwich on a preheated grill or frying pan. When sandwich grills to a golden brown, turn and brown second side.
9. Cut sandwich in half on the diagonal and place on serving plate.
10. Garnish with dill pickle wedge.

STEAK 'N CHEESE SANDWICH

Chipped Beef Steak, frozen	2½ oz. or As Desired
Salt	To Taste
White Pepper	To Taste
Mozzarella Cheese	1 slice
Twist Roll	1 each
Oleo Margarine, softened	As Needed
Lettuce, shredded	2 tablespoons
Mayonnaise	1 tablespoon
YIELD:	1 serving

PREPARATION:
1. Spread twist roll with softened oleo margarine and grill until golden brown.
2. Place frozen chipped beef steak on a preheated skillet or fry pan and grill in a small amount of softened oleo margarine.
3. Season with salt and pepper to taste.
4. Turn chipped steak as soon as blood begins to show around the edge of meat (only a few seconds). Turn meat carefully to prevent tearing into pieces.
5. Place mozzarella cheese over meat and cook only a few seconds until cheese begins to soften. DO NOT OVERCOOK.
6. Spread bottom of grilled roll with ½ tablespoon of mayonnaise and the shredded lettuce.
7. Place meat and cheese over shredded lettuce with cheese side facing up.
8. Spread top of grilled roll with remaining ½ tablespoon of mayonnaise.
9. Place top of roll on sandwich to close. Meat and cheese should hang slightly over edge of roll.

Beef Stew

MEATS

Perhaps better than any other section of our cookbook, the Meat recipes embody the changes the Hot Shoppes have undergone over the years. Some dishes date back to the early years—the Meat Loaf, for instance, has been on the menu for a long time, as have the Beef Stuffed Peppers with Tomato Sauce, which was among the first recipes developed for the Hot Shoppes. The Ham and Swiss Cheese Quiche, on the other hand, is a relatively new addition, and its popularity at dinner reflects the fact that many Americans today frequently order lighter entrees late in the day. In fact, most of the more recent recipes feature lighter sauces.

The variety of these dishes also mirrors the growth of Marriott Corporation, with hotels throughout the United States and the world. Chicken Fried Beefsteak with Gravy proudly represents the Lone Star State, BBQ Country Spare Ribs honor Dixie, and our European friends would be quite comfortable with Beef Stroganoff and Swedish Meatballs.

The Beef or Veal Stew combines the old and the new. In the early years, the stew was made only in its beef form. As the Hot Shoppes added other veal items to the menu, our chefs experimented with a veal alternative, and discovered that a similar blend of vegetables and spices produced an entirely distinctive flavor profile: sweeter and more aromatic. So we've included the recipe that accommodates both versions.

BEEF STEW

Beef Cubes, raw—1" cubes	3 cups
Oleo Margarine	1 tablespoon + 1 teaspoon
Garlic Clove, minced	⅓ teaspoon
Onion, ¼" dice	1 tablespoon
Beef Stock	2 cups
Gravy	2 cups

VEGETABLES FOR STEW

Carrots, raw—1" slice	1 cup
Onions, raw—1" dice	1½ cups
Celery, raw—1" dice	1 cup
Potatoes, raw and peeled—1" dice	1 cup
Water, cold	⅔ cup
Salt	1 teaspoon

TO MAKE GRAVY

Stock from Meat	2 cups
Oleo Margarine	2 tablespoons + 1 teaspoon
Flour, all purpose	¼ cup
Tomato Puree	¼ cup
Worcestershire Sauce	¼ teaspoon
Salt	To Taste
White Pepper	To Taste
YIELD:	6 to 8 servings

PREPARATION:
1. Melt 1 tablespoon plus 1 teaspoon of oleo margarine in a roasting pan. Add raw beef cubes, stirring to coat meat with melted oleo margarine.
2. Add minced garlic and chopped onion. Stir to blend with meat.
3. Place in a preheated 400° F oven to brown for 15 minutes. Stir meat cubes thoroughly and continue browning an additional 15 minutes.
4. Pour 2 cups of beef stock over browned beef cubes. Cover *tightly* with aluminum foil and roast in stock for 1 hour or until beef cubes are tender.
5. Drain stock from cooked beef cubes; reserve and measure for gravy.
6. Place carrots, onions, celery and potatoes in a medium size sauce pan. Dissolve salt in cold water and add to vegetables. Cover.
7. Bring to a boil, reduce heat and simmer just until vegetables are tender. DO NOT OVERCOOK.

8. TO MAKE GRAVY:
   - Melt oleo margarine. Add flour, stirring until well blended.
   - Add the stock from the meat, tomato puree, Worcestershire sauce, salt and white pepper to taste.
   - Cook, over low heat, stirring constantly until thickened, approximately 10 minutes. Stir so that no flour accumulates and that full thickening power is obtained.
9. Add gravy to meat cubes.
10. Drain cooked vegetables and add to hot meat and gravy, stirring well to gently combine.
11. Serve as desired over buttered noodles or buttermilk biscuits.

NOTE:
- Veal may be substituted for beef if Veal Stew is desired.
- Beef Stew may be topped with a pastry crust for Beef Pot Pie.

If desired, peas may be added to beef stew for added color and visual identity.

BEEF STUFFED PEPPERS WITH SAVORY TOMATO SAUCE

Ground Beef	*1 pound (approximately 2 cups)*
Onions, ¼" dice	*1¾ cups*
Celery, ¼" dice	*1¾ cups*
Mushrooms, ¼" slice	*½ cup*
Oleo margarine	*1 tablespoon + 2 teaspoons*
Red Pepper or Pimiento, ¼" dice	*3 tablespoons*
Salt	*To Taste*
White Pepper	*To Taste*
Thick Cream Sauce	*⅔ cup*
Green Pepper, halved lengthwise with seeds removed	*6 to 8 halves*
Water, cold	*1½ cups*
Bread Crumbs, buttered	*Optional*
Savory Tomato Sauce	*As Needed*

YIELD: *6 to 8 servings*

PREPARATION:
1. Prepare Cream Sauce according to instructions on recipe card.
2. Sauté ground beef in a frying pan, turning and breaking meat apart while cooking. Drain off excess fat.
3. Sauté onions, celery and mushrooms in oleo margarine until tender, but not browned.

4. Add the sautéed vegetables to the meat and continue cooking. Add the diced red pepper or pimiento, salt and white pepper to taste and the Cream Sauce.
5. Place green pepper halves in a covered sauce pan with 1 cup of cold water. Bring to a boil, reduce heat and simmer for 3 minutes. DO NOT OVERCOOK. They should be firm and green.
6. Divide ground beef mixture evenly among pepper halves. Arrange stuffed peppers in a baking dish or casserole large enough to hold the number of peppers prepared. Place ½ cup of water in the bottom of the baking dish.
7. Place buttered bread crumbs on top of each stuffed pepper half.
8. Bake in a preheated 350°F oven until hot and lightly browned on top, approximately 20 minutes.
9. Just before serving, top pepper halves with Savory Tomato Sauce.
10. Garnish with parsley or watercress.

MEATBALLS IN SWEET AND SOUR SAUCE

Onion, ¼" dice	*1½ cups*
Garlic, finely chopped	*½ teaspoon*
Oleo Margarine	*2 teaspoons*
Ground Beef	*2 pounds*
Bread Crumbs	*1 cup*
White Pepper	*⅜ teaspoon*
Salt	*1¼ teaspoons*
Egg, large – beaten	*1 each*
Sweet and Sour Sauce	*1 quart*
YIELD:	*6 to 8 servings*

PREPARATION:
1. Melt oleo margarine. Add onion and garlic; sauté lightly, approximately 5 minutes. Add white pepper and salt. Stir to blend.
2. In a medium size mixing bowl, combine hamburger, bread crumbs and beaten egg. Add sautéed vegetables. Mix well.
3. Shape mixture into meatballs, using approximately 2 tablespoons for each meatball.
4. Sauté meatballs in a skillet or on a greased baking tray and bake in a preheated 375°F oven until lightly browned and thoroughly cooked, approximately 25 minutes. DO NOT OVERCOOK. Discard excess fat.
5. Place cooked meatballs in a medium size casserole dish. Top with 1 quart Sweet and Sour Sauce. Stir gently to cover all meatballs with sauce.
6. Cover with aluminum foil and bake in a preheated 375°F oven until bubbling hot, approximately 20 minutes.
7. Serve over rice or noodles as desired.

SWEDISH MEATBALLS WITH ONION GRAVY

Onions, ¼" dice	*¾ cup*
Oleo Margarine	*1 tablespoon*
Brown Sugar	*1 tablespoon*
Salt	*¼ teaspoon*
White Pepper	*To Taste*
Allspice, ground	*¼ teaspoon*
Sage, ground	*2½ teaspoons*
Fresh Parsley, finely chopped	*¼ cup*
Bread Crumbs, fresh	*⅔ cup*
Ground Beef	*1¼ pounds*
Egg, large—beaten	*1 each*
Milk	*2 tablespoons*
Onion Gravy	*1½ quarts*
YIELD:	*6 to 8 servings*

PREPARATION:
1. Sauté diced onion in oleo margarine until tender, but not brown.
2. Add brown sugar, salt, white pepper to taste, allspice and sage to the sautéed onions. Stir to blend well.
3. Add onion mixture with finely chopped parsley and fresh bread crumbs to the ground beef.
4. Beat egg with 2 tablespoons of milk and add to the ground beef. Mix all ingredients until well blended and thoroughly combined.
5. Shape mixture into meatballs, using approximately 2 tablespoons for each meatball.
6. Sauté meatballs in a skillet or place on a greased baking tray and bake in a preheated 375° F oven until lightly browned and thoroughly cooked, approximately 25 minutes. DO NOT OVERCOOK. Discard excess fat.
7. Placed cooked meatballs in a medium size casserole dish. Top with 1½ quarts of Onion Gravy. Stir gently to cover all meatballs with sauce.
8. Cover with aluminum foil and bake in a preheated 375° F oven until bubbling hot, approximately 20 minutes.
9. Serve over rice or noodles as desired.

BEEF STUFFED CABBAGE WITH TOMATO SAUCE

Ground Beef	*¾ pound*
Onions, ¼" dice	*1⅓ cups*
Celery, ¼" dice	*1⅓ cups*
Mushrooms, ¼" dice	*1 cup*
Oleo Margarine	*2 tablespoons*
Red Pepper or Pimiento, ¼" dice	*¼ cup*
Salt	*To Taste*
White Pepper	*To Taste*
Thick Cream Sauce	*½ cup*
Cabbage Leaves	*12 each*
Water, cold	*½ cup*
Tomato Sauce, heated	*3 cups*

YIELD: *6 to 8 servings*

PREPARATION:

1. Sauté ground beef in a frying pan, turning and breaking meat apart while cooking. Drain off excess fat.
2. Sauté onion, celery and mushrooms in oleo margarine until tender, but not browned.
3. Add the sautéed vegetables to the meat and continue cooking. Add the diced red pepper or pimiento, salt and white pepper to taste and cream sauce.
4. Wash and core cabbage. Insert a large roasting fork in the center where the core was removed.
5. Place cabbage in boiling water, hold for 5 minutes. As cabbage starts to cook, remove outer leaves; continue blanching cabbage and taking off leaves until 12 usable leaves are obtained.
6. Divide ground beef mixture evenly among cabbage leaves. Fold bottom of leaf over filling; fold over sides of each leaf and roll up. If desired, cabbage rolls can be prepared to this point, held covered under refrigeration until needed for service.
7. Arrange stuffed cabbage with seam side down in a baking dish or casserole large enough to hold the number of cabbage rolls prepared. Place ½ cup of water in the bottom of the baking dish.
8. Cover pan tightly with aluminum foil. Bake in a preheated 350°F oven until thoroughly heated, approximately 40 minutes.
9. Just before serving, top stuffed cabbage rolls with Tomato Sauce.
10. Garnish with parsley or watercress.

MEAT LOAF

Onion, ¼" dice	1½ cups
Celery, ¼" dice	1½ cups
Oleo Margarine	1½ tablespoons
Salt	½ teaspoon
White Pepper	¼ teaspoon
Fresh Bread Crumbs	1⅓ cups
Egg, large – beaten	2 each
Ground Beef	2½ pounds
YIELD:	6 to 8 servings

PREPARATION:
1. Sauté diced onion and celery in oleo margarine until tender, but not browned.
2. Add salt and pepper to sautéed vegetables.
3. Combine sautéed vegetable mixture and bread crumbs with meat.
4. Add beaten eggs to meat mixture and mix until thoroughly combined.
5. Grease a 9" x 5" x 3" loaf pan. Cut wax paper to fit the bottom of the pan.
6. Place meat mixture into loaf pan, pressing mixture into the corners and end of pan. Pat down until smooth on top.
7. Bake in a preheated 325° F oven until thoroughly cooked, approximately 45 minutes to 1 hour.

Meat loaf cuts best when allowed to stand for approximately 15 minutes before serving.

SICILIAN CHOPPED STEAK

Ground Beef	*1⅓ pounds*
Egg, large — beaten	*1 each*
Green Pepper, finely chopped	*⅓ cup*
Onion, finely chopped	*⅓ cup*
Crushed Oregano	*Dash*
Pancake Flour	*½ cup*
Salt	*To Taste*
White Pepper	*⅛ teaspoon*
Worcestershire Sauce	*1½ teaspoons*
Tomato Juice	*⅓ cup*
Mushroom Caps, sautéed	*6 each*

Catsup Sauce	
Catsup	*2 tablespoons*
Oleo Margarine	*1 tablespoon*

YIELD: *6 servings*

PREPARATION:
1. Combine ground beef with beaten egg.
2. Add green pepper, chopped onion, oregano and pancake flour.
3. Combine salt, white pepper, Worcestershire sauce and tomato juice; add to mixture. Mix just until ingredients are completely blended.
4. Divide mixture into 6 equal portions, forming each into an oval shape.
5. Place in a greased baking pan and bake in a preheated 400° F oven for 20 to 30 minutes.
6. Prepare sauce: melt oleo margarine, add catsup; blend and hold warm until time of service.
7. Top each portion with 1 teaspoon of catsup sauce and 1 sautéed mushroom.

SALISBURY STEAK

Onions, ¼" dice	*⅓ cup*
Oleo Margarine	*1 tablespoon*
Salt	*¼ teaspoon*
White Pepper	*¼ teaspoon*
Chicken Base	*1½ teaspoons*
Water, cold	*¾ cup*
Ground Beef	*1¾ pounds*
Live Bread Crumbs	*1½ cups*
Gravy or Sauce	*As Desired*
YIELD:	*6 to 8 servings*

PREPARATION:
1. Sauté onions in oleo margarine until tender, but not browned.
2. Add salt and white pepper to the sautéed onions.
3. Dissolve chicken base in water.
4. Combine ground beef, bread crumbs, onion mixture and chicken base dissolved in water. Mix just enough to thoroughly combine.
5. Divide salisbury steak mixture into 6 to 8 equal portions.
6. Place in a frying pan and fry over a moderately low heat until meat turns pink and becomes juicy around the edges.
7. Turn meat and continue cooking until done. Turn only once. Do not press with a spatula while cooking.
8. Serve with gravy or sauce as desired.

CHICKEN FRIED BEEFSTEAK WITH GRAVY

Cube Steaks, fresh	*6 to 8 each*
Flour, all purpose	*1½ cups*
Salt	*4 teaspoons*
Paprika	*4 teaspoons*
Black Pepper	*½ teaspoon*
Oleo Margarine	*6 to 8 tablespoons*
Gravy	*As Needed*
Fresh Parsley, finely chopped	*As Needed*
YIELD:	*6 to 8 servings*

PREPARATION:
1. Combine flour, salt, paprika and pepper to make a seasoned flour mixture. Mix thoroughly to combine.
2. Melt oleo margarine in a large frying pan over medium heat.
3. Coat each steak with seasoned flour mixture.
4. Place floured steaks in frying pan and fry until thoroughly cooked and well browned on both sides. Turn only one time.
5. Serve Chicken Fried Beefsteak with gravy.
6. Garnish with finely chopped parsley.

NOTE: Do not place floured steaks on top of each other prior to frying.

BEEF TURNOVER WITH GRAVY

Roast Beef, cooked — ¼" dice or Ground Beef, raw	1 cup (½ pound)
Onion, ¼" dice	1 cup
Celery, ¼" dice	1 cup
Mushrooms, ¼" dice	½ cup
Cream Sauce	½ cup
Salt	¼ teaspoon
White Pepper	⅛ teaspoon
Oleo Margarine (when cooked Roast Beef is used)	1 tablespoon
Gravy	As Needed
Pie Dough	1 recipe
YIELD:	4 to 6 servings

PREPARATION:
1. *Ground Beef* — Sauté meat, omitting oleo margarine; turn and break meat apart while cooking. Add raw vegetables; cover and cook until vegetables are tender.
   Cooked Roast Beef — Sauté vegetables in oleo margarine until tender, but not browned. Add cooked, diced roast beef.
2. Add cream sauce.
3. Add salt and pepper. Adjust seasonings as desired.
4. Cover and chill mixture before making turnovers.
5. Prepare pie dough for a two crust pie according to recipe; roll dough ⅛" thick and cut into approximate 6" diameter circles.
6. Wet half of rim of each dough circle with cold water. Place approximately 2½ tablespoons of filling mixture in center of circle and spread *slightly*.
7. Fold dough over to make a turnover and seal edges securely with a fork; prick top of turnover with a fork to allow steam to escape while baking and prevent crust from becoming soggy. Brush with melted oleo margarine.

Beef turnover with gravy

8. Place on a greased baking pan and bake in a preheated 350°F oven to a golden brown, approximately 25 to 30 minutes.
9. Serve with gravy as desired.

BEEF STROGANOFF

Beef Tenderloin Tips	*4 cups*
Oleo Margarine	*9 tablespoons + 1 teaspoon*
Onions, ¼" dice	*¾ cup*
Mushrooms, sliced ⅛"	*2½ cups*
Garlic Clove, finely chopped	*1 each*
White Pepper	*To Taste*
Salt	*¼ teaspoon*
Paprika	*⅓ teaspoon*
Chicken Stock	*2⅔ cups*
Flour, all purpose	*5 tablespoons*
Oleo Margarine, softened	*4 tablespoons*
Sour Cream	*1 cup*
YIELD:	*4 to 6 servings*

PREPARATION:
1. Sauté garlic in 8 tablespoons of oleo margarine.
2. Add onions, mushrooms, salt, white pepper and paprika and sauté lightly.
3. Place 1 tablespoon plus 1 teaspoon of oleo margarine in a frying pan. Add beef tips and sauté well.
4. Remove meat with a slotted spoon and hold. Brown remaining liquid in frying pan. Do not burn. Drain off fat.
5. Add chicken stock. Bring to a boil, stirring to dissolve browned liquid. Reduce heat to a simmer.
6. In a small skillet, melt 4 tablespoons of oleo margarine. Add flour, stirring until well blended.
7. Combine oleo/flour mixture with simmering stock. Simmer until thickened, about 5 minutes.
8. Combine heated mixture with sour cream as close to service as possible—adding a small amount of sauce to sour cream, stirring well. Gradually stir sour cream mixture into sauce and blend well. *Do not* allow mixture to boil after sour cream is added.
9. Add meat and onion/mushroom mixture to sauce and stir well. Heat and serve. DO NOT BOIL.
10. If Stroganoff is not served immediately, hold on a double boiler set up until time of service.
11. Serve with noodles or rice as desired.

BREADED VEAL CUTLET WITH FRICASSEE SAUCE

Veal Cutlets, fresh	*6 to 8 each*
Onion Juice	*3 to 4 teaspoons*
Salt	*To Taste*
White Pepper	*To Taste*
Flour, all purpose	*2½ cups*
Eggs, large – beaten	*4 each*
Water, cold	*1 cup*
Bread Crumbs	*3 cups*
Fricassee Sauce	*As Needed*
YIELD:	*6 to 8 servings*

PREPARATION:
1. Sprinkle veal cutlets with onion juice, sprinkling approximately ½ teaspoon of juice on each veal cutlet. Season with salt and white pepper.
2. Make egg wash by thoroughly combining beaten egg and cold water.
3. Dip one cutlet at a time into flour; then in egg wash, then in bread crumbs.

4. Fry breaded cutlets in a frying pan in preheated 325° F vegetable oil until golden brown on all sides and thoroughly cooked, approximately 5 to 6 minutes.
5. Remove cutlets from pan and place on a wire rack placed in a baking pan. Cover and bake in a preheated 325° F oven for 10 minutes.
6. Serve with Fricassee Sauce.

BARBEQUE COUNTRY SPARE RIBS

Country Spare Ribs, pork—portioned as desired	*7 pounds*
Salt	*To Taste*
White Pepper	*To Taste*
Barbeque Sauce	*3 cups*
Fricassee Sauce	*1 cup*
YIELD:	*6 to 8 servings*

PREPARATION:
1. Prepare Barbeque and Fricassee Sauces according to instructions given on individual recipes.
2. Sprinkle country spare ribs with salt and white pepper to taste.
3. Place spare ribs in a roasting pan. Do not cover.
4. Bake in a preheated 350° F oven until ribs are browned, approximately ½ hour. Drain off the fat which has accumulated in the pan and discard.
5. Combine Barbeque and Fricassee Sauces and pour evenly over each portion.
6. Cover pan with aluminum foil and bake in a preheated 350° F oven for 1½ hours or until ribs are very tender. Baste with sauce several times during baking.

BAKED HAM WITH ORANGE RAISIN SAUCE

Ham, fully cooked — boneless preferred	8 to 10 pounds
Cloves, whole	As Needed

ORANGE RAISIN SAUCE

Raisins, seedless	1 cup
Orange Juice	3¼ cups
Sugar, granulated	½ cup + 2 tablespoons
Cinnamon, ground	⅛ teaspoon
Cloves, ground	⅛ teaspoon
Cornstarch	3 tablespoons

YIELD:

PREPARATION:
1. Score fat side of ham into ¾" rectangles.
2. Stick one each whole clove in the center of each rectangle.
3. Place ham in a roasting pan fat side up with an oven proof thermometer inserted in the center of ham. Add 1 cup of water to pan.
4. Bake in a preheated 325°F oven until internal temperature reaches 90° to 100°F.
5. If ends of ham begin to burn, cover loosely with a small piece of aluminum foil. Watch carefully to keep from burning, as it burns easily.
6. Cook to 130°F internal temperature.
7. To Make Orange Raisin Sauce:
   - Check raisins to remove any stems and soak for ½ hour in 3 cups of orange juice.
   - Bring raisins and juice to a boil and add granulated sugar, cinnamon and cloves; reduce heat to a simmer.
   - Combine ¼ cup of orange juice with cornstarch and blend until thoroughly combined.
   - Stir cornstarch mixture into simmering raisins and cook, stirring constantly, until mixture is thick and clear, approximately 10 minutes.
   - Hold on a double boiler set up until time of service.
8. Serve slice ham topped with Orange Raisin Sauce.

HAM AND SWISS CHEESE QUICHE

Eggs, large – beaten	2 each
Mayonnaise	½ cup
Milk	½ cup
Cornstarch	1 tablespoon
Swiss Cheese, shredded	2¼ cups
Spring Onions, ¼ " slice	⅓ cup
Ham, ¼ " dice	1 cup
White Pepper	⅛ teaspoon
Pie Shell with Rim (10" diameter) – unbaked	1 each
YIELD:	6 servings

PREPARATION:
1. Beat eggs well. Add mayonnaise, milk, cornstarch and white pepper. Continue beating to blend well.
2. Add grated Swiss cheese, onions and diced ham. Blend well. Cover and keep refrigerated until time of use.
3. Stir mixture to combine and place in the unbaked 10" diameter pie shell.
4. Place quiche on a cookie sheet or baking tray and bake in a preheated 400°F oven for 35 to 40 minutes or until a knife inserted in center comes out clean.
5. Allow quiche to set approximately 8 minutes before cutting.
6. Cut each 10" quiche into 6 equal wedges.
7. Garnish with parsley and cherry tomatoes, if desired.

Maryland Style Fried Chicken

POULTRY

As with any dish that a region claims to be its own, to be one of its emblems, there are as many recipes for "Southern Fried Chicken" as there are southern cooks. We tried to narrow the field a little, by calling our version Maryland Style Fried Chicken.

Hot Shoppes' Baked Chicken Southern Style with Cornbread Dressing is one of our longest names, authentically Southern, and takes a relatively long time to prepare, because the cornbread dressing should be made from scratch. Which means that you must bake your own cornbread to use as the main ingredient of the dressing. There's no other way to achieve the distinctive flavor, and the process is involved...but it's worth it.

Like the Baked Chicken, most of the other poultry dishes take a substantial amount of time to prepare. The croquettes, for instance, require that a whole chicken be boiled, and afterwards that the meat be carefully picked and diced. These time consuming tasks remind us of how traditional these dishes actually are. They recall earlier days, before the advent of flash freezing and microwaves. Perhaps it's because of such traditional associations that our Fricassee Chicken with Dumplings is most in demand on Mother's Day—even more so now, than in years past.

MARYLAND-STYLE FRIED CHICKEN

Flour, all purpose	*1½ cups*
Salt	*4 teaspoons*
Paprika	*4 teaspoons*
Pepper, Black—coarsely ground	*½ teaspoon*
Eggs, large—beaten	*2 each*
Water, cold	*½ cup*
Flour, all purpose	*As Needed*
Chicken—2½ to 3 pound broiler—fryer, cut up	*1 each*
Vegetable Oil for Frying	*As Needed*
YIELD:	*4 servings*

PREPARATION:
1. Combine flour and seasonings in a shallow pan. Stir to blend well.
2. Make egg wash: combine 2 beaten eggs and ½ cup of water until ingredients are thoroughly moistened.
3. Add chicken, 2 or 3 pieces at a time to seasoned flour mixture and turn to coat all sides.
4. Dip floured chicken in egg wash and then in seasoned flour.
5. Heat vegetable oil. Brown meaty pieces of chicken first, then add other pieces. Don't crowd—you may want to use two skillets.
6. Brown chicken on one side, turn and brown on second side.
7. When chicken is lightly browned, reduce heat and cover tightly.
8. Cook chicken until tender, approximately 20 to 40 minutes.
9. Uncover chicken during the last 10 minutes of cooking time to allow chicken to crisp.

NOTE:
— If desired, chicken may be deep fried in a preheated 350°F fryer or deep electric skillet, until chicken is tender and cooked throughout. This method will produce a crispier product.
— Many variations of fried chicken have been developed over the years. This recipe reflects one of the more popular. Our current recipe is being produced and served by several Divisions of Marriott Corporation and is available for your enjoyment in our restaurants. Bon Appetit!

CHICKEN CROQUETTES

Chicken, cooked, skinned and deboned — ¼" dice	*2 cups*
Celery, ¼" dice	*¾ cup*
Onion, ¼" dice	*¾ cup*
Oleo Margarine	*3 tablespoons*
Eggs, large — beaten	*2 each*
Live Bread Crumbs	*⅔ cup*
Salt	*⅛ teaspoon*
White Pepper	*⅛ teaspoon*
Poultry Seasoning	*⅛ teaspoon*
Thick Fricassee Sauce	*¼ cup*
Flour, all purpose	*As Needed*
Water, cold	*¼ cup*

YIELD: *4 to 6 servings*

PREPARATION:
1. Sauté celery and onion in oleo margarine until tender, but not browned. DO NOT OVERCOOK.
2. Combine diced chicken, bread crumbs and sautéed vegetables.
3. Add the salt, pepper and poultry seasoning to the Fricassee Sauce.
4. Add 1 beaten egg and Fricassee Sauce to the chicken mixture and stir to blend well.
5. Cover and refrigerate. Chill mixture thoroughly before making into croquettes.
6. Divide mixture into 8 to 10 equal portions.
7. Mix remaining beaten egg with ¼ cup of cold water to make egg wash.
8. Shape each portion into a cylindrical shape. Roll in flour and then dip in egg wash.
9. Dip in bread crumbs to coat all sides.
10. Deep fry in a preheated 350°F fryer until golden brown and heated throughout, approximately 3 to 3½ minutes.
11. Top croquettes with additional Fricassee Sauce when served.

FRICASSEE CHICKEN AND DUMPLINGS

Chicken, cooked, skinned and deboned — ½" dice	*4 cups*
Fricassee Sauce, hot	*1½ quarts*
Dumplings	*12 each*
YIELD:	*6 servings*

PREPARATION:
1. Place diced chicken evenly over the bottom half of a 9" x 12" oblong baking dish.
2. Add 1½ quarts of hot Fricassee Sauce. Heat in a 350°F oven until *bubbling* hot.
3. Prepare dumplings according to instructions on dumpling recipe.
4. Place dumplings over top of Fricassee Sauce mixture.
5. Cover tightly with aluminum foil and bake in a preheated 350°F oven until dumplings are done, approximately 20 minutes.

NOTE:
— If desired, raw biscuit dough may be used in place of dumplings. Bake biscuits uncovered in a preheated 350°F oven until biscuits are golden brown and cooked throughout, approximately 12 to 15 minutes.

BAKED CHICKEN SOUTHERN STYLE

Cut Chicken	*16 pieces*
or	
Chicken Quarters	*8 each*
Oleo Margarine, softened	*As Needed*
Salt	*To Taste*
White Pepper	*To Taste*
Cornbread Dressing	*Double Recipe*
YIELD:	*8 servings*

PREPARATION:
1. Prepare cornbread dressing according to instructions on recipe.
2. Place cornbread dressing in a well greased baking pan.

3. Wash chickens and drain thoroughly. Sprinkle with salt and white pepper. Let stand for 10 minutes.
4. Rub chicken with softened oleo margarine and place chicken, skin side up on top of cornbread dressing.
5. Place chicken and dressing in a preheated 375°F oven for 35 minutes—turn chicken over and continue cooking for 20 minutes—return chicken to skin side up position and continue cooking for an additional 10 minutes to brown any dressing that sticks to the chicken. Test chicken to assure that it is thoroughly cooked before serving.
6. Serve with gravy as desired.

SAUTÉED CHICKEN LIVERS

Chicken Livers, raw—frozen	*3½ pounds*
Salt	*To Taste*
White Pepper	*To Taste*
Flour, all purpose	*As Needed*
Oleo Margarine	*As Needed*
YIELD:	*6 to 8 servings*

PREPARATION:
1. Remove chicken livers from freezer and allow to thaw under refrigeration for 24 hours prior to service.
2. Wash chicken livers and drain well.
3. Cut each liver in half and season with salt and white pepper to taste.
4. Dredge lightly with flour and sauté in a small amount of oleo margarine, over low heat until tender and golden brown.
5. Serve sautéed chicken livers over rice topped with Fricassee Sauce if desired.

CHICKEN CACCIATORE

Chicken Quarters	6 to 8 each
Vegetable Oil	As Needed
Onion, ¼" dice	2½ cups
Garlic, minced	1 teaspoon
Oleo Margarine	6 tablespoons
Tomatoes, canned	4 cups
Tomato Puree	½ cup
Chicken Stock	1⅓ cups
Dry White Wine	½ cup
Sugar, granulated	½ teaspoon
Salt	1¼ teaspoons
White Pepper	To Taste
Oregano	2 teaspoons
Bay Leaf	1 each
Green Pepper, 1" dice	⅔ cup
Mushrooms, ¼" slice	1 cup

YIELD: 6 to 8 servings

PREPARATION:
— SAUCE
1. Drain tomatoes, reserving juice. Cut tomatoes into ¼" dice.
2. Melt oleo margarine in a medium size sauce pan; add onion and garlic and sauté for 5 minutes.
3. Add diced tomatoes, the reserved juice, tomato puree, chicken stock, white wine, sugar, salt, white pepper, oregano and bay leaf. Stir well to blend.
4. Bring to a boil; reduce heat and simmer covered for 30 minutes.
— CHICKEN
5. Wash chicken under cold running water. Discard excess fat. Drain thoroughly.
6. Sprinkle lightly with salt and pepper.
7. Brown chicken on all sides in a small amount of vegetable oil.

Note: Do not dredge chicken in flour.

Chicken cacciatore

— ASSEMBLY FOR BAKING
8. Place one half of sauce in the bottom of a roasting pan.
9. Cover sauce with chicken quarters.
10. Sprinkle chicken with diced green peppers and sliced mushrooms.
11. Top with remaining half of sauce.
12. Cover with aluminum foil and bake in a preheated 375° F oven for approximately 60 to 75 minutes or until chicken is done.
13. Hold chicken covered until time of service.
14. Garnish with finely chopped parsley.

NOTE:
— Many variations of Chicken Cacciatore have been developed over the years. This recipe reflects the current one being prepared in our restaurants.

Macaroni au Gratin

CASSEROLES

The history of Hot Shoppes' casseroles is a history of creativity and adaptability—which is, of course, what casseroles are all about: the combining of convenient, healthy items into new mixtures of flavor. Our soufflés came about as an adaption to the meat rationing of World War II; Mr. Marriott asked our chefs to develop entrees with those ingredients not subject to the most severe rationing, and soufflés were the popular solution. So popular, in fact, that we kept them on the menu long after the rationing ended.

Our Monterey Jack Vegetable Bake has been a favorite since its inception, especially in the Washington area where there is a large community of Seventh Day Adventists, for whom vegetarianism is a religious practice. This recipe has also been in demand as a way to entice youngsters into eating vegetables; *Bon Appetit Magazine* responded to just such a request by reprinting it in their "R.S.V.P. Column" for the July, 1980 issue.

Although casseroles present frugal cooks an opportunity to make the most of fresh odds-and-ends, there are also firmly traditional casserole dishes, for which we advise you follow the recipes very closely. Chief among those dishes are the Hot Shoppes' Macaroni Au Gratin, and Chicken Pot Pie.

MACARONI AU GRATIN

MACARONI:

Water	1½ quarts
Salt	1½ teaspoons
Elbow Macaroni	½ pound

CHEESE SAUCE:

Oleo Margarine	3 tablespoons
Flour, all purpose	⅓ cup
White Pepper	Dash
Milk	3⅓ cups
Salt	Dash
Sharp Cheddar Cheese, shredded	1½ cups

CHEESE TOPPING:

Flour, all purpose	1 tablespoon + 1 teaspoon
Paprika	½ teaspoon
Oleo Margarine, well-chilled	1 tablespoon
Sharp Cheddar Cheese, shredded	⅓ cup
YIELD:	6 to 8 servings

PREPARATION:
1. Add salt to water and bring to a boil in a three quart sauce pan.
2. Add macaroni and cook until tender, approximately 10 to 12 minutes. Stir several times during cooking to prevent sticking.
3. Drain macaroni and rinse with cold water.

CHEESE SAUCE:
4. Melt oleo margarine in a two quart sauce pan over low heat.
5. Blend in flour and white pepper. Cook at least two minutes, stirring continuously while cooking.
6. Slowly add milk, continuing to stir until sauce thickens.
7. Add salt and shredded cheese; stir *just* until cheese is melted. Overheating will cause the sauce to break down.

CHEESE TOPPING:
8. Mix flour with paprika.
9. Combine shredded cheese, well-chilled oleo margarine and flour mixture *just* until crumbly. If overworked, the mixture will form a paste.

ASSEMBLY AND BAKING:
10. Add the cooked, drained macaroni to the Cheese Sauce; stir well to blend.
11. Turn mixture into a well-greased two quart casserole.
12. Sprinkle evenly with Cheese Topping.
13. Bake in a preheated 350° F oven until golden brown and heated through, approximately 25-35 minutes.

NOTE:
— Cooked and drained macaroni can be covered and refrigerated for later use if not combined with Cheese Sauce right away.

Mix cooked and drained macaroni with cheese sauce just prior to baking.

CHEESE SOUFFLÉ

Sharp Cheese, shredded	3 cups
Eggs, large	9 each
Oleo Margarine	6 tablespoons
Flour, all purpose	¼ cup + 2 tablespoons
Milk	2¼ cups
Salt	1½ teaspoons
Dry Mustard	⅜ teaspoon
Cayenne Pepper	⅛ teaspoon
White Pepper	⅛ teaspoon
YIELD:	6 to 8 servings

PREPARATION:
1. Melt oleo margarine in a medium size sauce pan.
2. Add flour and blend thoroughly.
3. Add milk and bring to a boil. Boil 1 minute.
4. Remove from heat and add salt, dry mustard, cayenne and white peppers and shredded cheese.
5. Separate eggs into whites and yolks.
6. Beat egg yolks until light in color and smooth.
7. Stir ¼ cup hot cheese mixture into beaten egg yolks, then blend the remaining cheese mixture with egg yolks.
8. Beat egg whites until stiff. Fold hot mixture into egg whites *very slowly*.
9. Pour into a greased 8″ x 11″ baking pan or glass dish.

10. Place pan in a larger pan filled with water to a depth of 1 inch.
11. Bake uncovered in a preheated 300°F oven until a knife inserted in center comes out clean, approximately 1 hour and 15 minutes.
12. Serve topped with Cheese or Tomato Sauce as desired.

Note: Do not beat egg whites ahead of time. They will lose their volume and the soufflé will not rise to its full height.

MONTEREY JACK VEGETABLE BAKE

Onions, ¼" dice	*1¾ cups*
Carrots, ¼" slice	*2 cups*
Broccoli, fresh—1" pieces	*7 cups*
Oleo Margarine	*2 tablespoons + 1 teaspoon*
Soy Sauce	*3 tablespoons + 2 teaspoons*
Salt	*¾ teaspoon*
White Pepper	*¼ teaspoon*
Dill Weed	*¼ teaspoon + ⅛ teaspoon*
Celery Seed	*½ teaspoon + ⅛ teaspoon*
Garlic, minced	*1¼ teaspoons*
Eggs, large—beaten	*6 each*
Milk	*1⅓ cups*
Monterey Jack Cheese, shredded	*4 cups*
YIELD:	*6 to 8 servings*

PREPARATION:
1. Wash and cut off tops of broccoli to make small florets. Set aside. Peel outside stems of broccoli to remove tough skin. Split stems in halves then in quarters, and cut in 1" lengths.
2. Sauté broccoli stems in melted oleo margarine for 3 minutes.
3. Add soy sauce, salt, white pepper, dill weed, celery seed, and minced garlic. Cook over medium heat for 5 minutes.
4. Add onions, carrots and broccoli florets. Cook just until vegetables are tender, approximately 12 minutes, stirring occasionally. Cool vegetables.
5. Blend beaten eggs with milk.
6. Add shredded Monterey Jack cheese. Blend well.
7. Combine the cooled vegetables with egg-milk-cheese mixture.

8. Pour vegetable mixture into a 3 quart casserole and place casserole in a pan with 1″ of hot water in the bottom of the pan.
9. Bake in a preheated 350° F oven until a knife inserted in the center comes out clean and the top is a golden brown, approximately 45 minutes to 1 hour.
10. Remove from oven and allow to set for several minutes before cutting.
11. Garnish with alfalfa sprouts, sliced mushrooms and black olives or as desired.

CHICKEN POT PIE

Carrots, peeled — ¼″ slice	1½ cups
Celery, ½″ dice	1⅓ cups
Salt	½ teaspoon
Water, cold	1 cup
Onion, ½″ dice	1 cup
Fricassee Sauce	3½ cups
Peas	¾ cup
Chicken, cooked, skinned and deboned — ½″ dice	3½ cups

PASTRY DOUGH

Flour, all purpose	¾ cup + 1 tablespoon
Baking Powder, double acting	1 teaspoon
Baking Soda	⅛ teaspoon
Salt	Dash
Shortening, firm	¼ cup
Buttermilk	⅓ cup
Oleo Margarine	As Needed

YIELD:	6 to 8 servings

PREPARATION:
1. Place sliced carrots and diced celery in a medium size saucepan. Add salt dissolved in cold water.
2. Bring to a boil. Cover, reduce heat and cook 5 minutes.
3. Add onions to partially cooked vegetables. Continue cooking an additional 5 minutes, just until vegetables are tender. Do not overcook.
4. Drain cooked vegetables and set aside until needed.
5. Prepare Fricassee Sauce according to instructions given on recipe.
6. Thaw peas completely, but do not cook. Drain well.

chicken pot pie

7. Combine cooked vegetables, peas, diced chicken and Fricassee Sauce in a double boiler. Stir just enough to combine. Heat thoroughly, but do not overcook.
8. Prepare Pastry Dough:
    — Sift together flour, salt, baking powder and soda.
    — Blend firm shortening with the flour mixture until mealy with particles the size of peas.
    — Add buttermilk all at once. Mix just enough to blend well.
    — Roll dough thin on a lightly floured board. Cut slightly larger than casserole shape. Cut a slit or prick top of pie with a fork to allow steam to escape during baking process.
9. Place hot pot pie mixture into casserole.
10. Moisten edges of casserole with water. Cover with crust. With thumb and forefinger, press crust to moistened edges of casserole.
11. Place casserole on a cookie sheet or baking pan. Bake in a preheated 350°F oven until golden brown, approximately 25 to 30 minutes.
12. If desired, brush top of pastry crust with melted oleo margarine.

NOTE:
— Pot pie mixture may also be used as Creamed Chicken and Vegetables if prepared without the pastry crust. Serve over biscuits or rice as desired.

CHICKEN TETRAZZINI

Water, cold	2 cups
Salt	2 teaspoons
Spaghetti	¼ pound
Mushrooms, sliced ¼ "	2 cups
Onion, ¼ " dice	½ cup
Green Pepper, ¼ " dice	¼ cup
Oleo Margarine	3 tablespoons
Fricassee Sauce	2½ cups
Chicken, cooked, skinned and deboned — ½ " dice	2 cups
Chicken Stock	¼ cup + 2 tablespoons
Bread Crumbs, buttered	As Needed

YIELD: 6 to 8 servings

PREPARATION:
1. Add salt to boiling water and bring to a boil in a three quart saucepan.
2. Break spaghetti twice and add to the boiling water. Stir to prevent sticking.
3. Cook until tender, approximately 11 to 12 minutes. Do not overcook. Drain and rinse with cold water.
4. Sauté diced mushrooms, onions and green peppers in oleo margarine, until tender but not browned.
5. Combine chicken stock with diced chicken and allow to set until most of stock is absorbed, about 30 minutes to 1 hour.
6. Combine all ingredients and place in a greased 2 quart casserole dish. Sprinkle with browned buttered bread crumbs.
7. Bake in a preheated 350° F oven for 20 minutes or until golden brown.

BEEF, MACARONI AND TOMATOES

MACARONI	
Water	*3 cups*
Salt	*¾ teaspoon*
Elbow Macaroni	*1 cup*

SAUCE	
Oleo Margarine	*2 tablespoons*
Ground Beef	*1 pound*
Onion, ¼″ dice	*¼ cup*
Tomatoes	*6 cups*
Salt	*1 teaspoon*
White Pepper	*¼ teaspoon*
Sugar, granulated	*1 tablespoon + ½ teaspoon*

YIELD:	*6 to 8 servings*

PREPARATION:

1. Add salt to water and bring to a boil in a medium size saucepan.
2. Add macaroni and cook until tender, approximately 10 to 12 minutes. Stir several times during cooking to prevent sticking.
3. Drain macaroni and rinse with cold water.

SAUCE

4. In a medium size frying pan, melt oleo margarine. Add ground beef and diced onion. Stir several times to break up meat. Cook only until no pink meat is visible. Drain off excess fat.
5. Chop tomatoes in 1″ pieces and add to meat mixture.
6. Add salt, white pepper and sugar. Simmer slowly until sauce begins to thicken, approximately 30 to 40 minutes.

ASSEMBLY AND BAKING

7. Mix cooked, well drained macaroni with sauce and place in casserole dish.
8. Bake uncovered in a preheated 350°F oven for 15 minutes to allow to set to proper consistency and mixture is heated thoroughly.

ESCALLOPED POTATOES WITH HAM

Potatoes, peeled, ¼" slice and cooked	4 cups
Onions, finely diced	⅓ cup
Oleo Margarine	5 tablespoons
Flour, all purpose	¼ cup + 1 tablespoon
Milk	3 cups
Salt	¼ teaspoon + ⅛ teaspoon
White Pepper	½ teaspoon
Ham, ⅜" dice or julienne cut	2 cups
Bread Crumbs, buttered	⅓ cup
YIELD:	*6 to 8 servings*

PREPARATION:
1. Sauté onions in 1 tablespoon of oleo margarine.
2. Melt remaining 4 tablespoons of oleo margarine. Add flour, stirring until flour is completely dissolved.
3. Add milk, salt and white pepper. Stir continuously until all ingredients are blended and mixture begins to thicken.
4. Combine sautéed onions, sliced potatoes and ham with the thickened sauce, stirring gently to blend.
5. Place mixture into a greased casserole dish and top with buttered bread crumbs.
6. Place casserole dish on a cookie sheet or baking pan to prevent spillage during baking.
7. Bake in a preheated 350°F oven until hot and bubbling around edges, approximately 40 minutes to 50 minutes.

NOTE:
— If potatoes are peeled and sliced before cooking, they can be sliced thinner and more evenly.

The sauce will have a creamier texture if the casserole dish is placed in a pan filled with water to the depth of 1", prior to baking.

Fried Fillet of Fish Almondine

FISH, SEAFOOD

Because the Hot Shoppes have always been based in the Washington area, we've always enjoyed access to some of the finest seafood in the world, such as blue crabs, oysters, bay scallops, and cherrystone clams. So we've always had many loyal seafood lovers among our clientele, and a great incentive for refining our fish and seafood dishes.

One rule dwarfs all others in preparing seafood recipes — freshness. All of our fish and seafood recipes will be greatly enhanced by the delicate flavors and tender textures of fresh ocean produce. That doesn't mean you have to be a fisherman to try these recipes, but it helps if you have a good seafood market nearby.

Our Breaded Shrimp has been widely requested for many years, even by those people who claim they "don't like fish." This is probably because we soak our shrimp in milk, which enhances their sweetness and eliminates the briny quality some diners might object to.

Fried Fillet of Fish Almondine also succeeds with a broad range of Hot Shoppes' regular customers, for two reasons: it has a distinctive appearance and texture, owing to the thick, cracker breading and the sliced almonds; it offers a subtle combination of the bittersweet almond, the fillet's sweetness, and the breading's light saltiness. As you try this recipe with different kinds of skinless fillet (flounder, sole, etc.), you'll discover interesting shadings of flavor, although you must remember to be very careful to avoid using too much of the strong almond extract.

FRIED FILLET OF FISH ALMONDINE

Fish Fillet, frozen and thawed or fresh — approx. 3–5 oz. net weight each	*6 each*
Flour, all purpose	*1 cup*
Salt	*To Taste*
White Pepper	*To Taste*
Eggs, large	*4 each*
Water, cold	*⅔ cup*
Pure Almond Extract	*1 tablespoon*
Saltine Crackers, crushed	*3 cups*
Almonds, sliced	*⅔ cup*
Frying Oil	*As Needed*
YIELD:	*6 portions*

PREPARATION:
1. Wash fish fillets and season with salt and white pepper to taste.

EGG WASH:
2. Beat whole eggs in a small mixing bowl until yolks and white are well blended. Add water and almond extract. Beat until well blended. Set aside in a 2½" deep baking pan or casserole dish.
3. Place all purpose flour in a second 2½" deep baking pan or casserole dish.
4. Coarsely crush saltine crackers into approximately ½" crumbs and mix with sliced almonds in a third 2½" deep baking pan or casserole dish.

BREADING PROCEDURE:
1. Bread only one portion of fish at a time.
2. Place each fillet in flour turning and pressing to coat all sides. Shake off excess flour.
3. Then dip each fillet in almond flavored egg mixture. The fillet will become sticky to touch.
4. Then dip each fillet in the cracker-almond mixture, pressing each fillet gently but firmly so that the mixture will adhere to the fish.
5. Place breaded fish fillets in a single layer on a plate or tray. Cover loosely with plastic film and hold refrigerated until ready to fry.

FRYING PROCEDURE:
1. Place frying oil in deep fat fryer to the depth recommended by the manufacturer in the instruction book *or* place 1" of frying oil in an electric skillet.
2. Preheat oil to 350°F.
3. Carefully place breaded fish fillets in preheated oil one at a time. Only fry as many at one time that will fit in the fryer or skillet without allowing fillets to touch each other.

4. Brown each fillet on one side. Turn carefully and brown other side. Fry a total of 5 to 7 minutes depending on the size of fish fillet.
5. Remove fillets from oil. Drain on paper towels or wire rack. Serve immediately for optimum quality.
6. Serve with tartar sauce, if desired.
7. Garnish with lemon wedge.

NOTE: *Any variety of boneless, skinless fish may be used in this recipe; however, flounder is preferred.*

BAKED STUFFED FILLET OF FISH

Dressing for Stuffed Fish	*1 recipe or As Needed*
Fillet of Fish, 6 oz. portions	*6 to 8 each*
Oleo Margarine, melted	*As Needed*
Salt	*To Taste*
White Pepper	*To Taste*
YIELD:	*6 to 8 servings*

PREPARATION:
1. Prepare dressing for stuffed fish according to instructions given on recipe.
2. Wash fish fillets and spread out flat.
3. Grease a shallow baking pan with melted oleo margarine.
4. Place 6 to 8 portions of dressing in pan using approximately ¼ cup for each portion. Allow enough space between portions so that fish fillets will barely touch one another when placed on top of stuffing—do not crowd together.
5. Brush each fillet with melted oleo margarine.
6. Season with salt and white pepper to taste.
7. Cover pan tightly with aluminum foil.
8. Bake in a preheated 350° F oven for approximately 20 minutes or until fish is done.
9. Serve with sauce as desired: Lemon Butter or Tomato Sauce.
10. Garnish with parsley and one lemon wedge.

FRENCH FRIED FILLET OF FISH

Fish Fillets, 5 to 6 oz. portions	*6 to 8 each*
Salt	*To Taste*
White Pepper	*To Taste*
Flour, all purpose	*1 cup*
Egg, large — beaten	*4 each*
Water, cold	*⅔ cup*
Live Bread Crumbs	*1 cup*
Vegetable Oil	*As Needed*

YIELD: *6 to 8 servings*

PREPARATION:
1. Wash fish fillets. Do not soak in water.
2. Season with salt and white pepper to taste.
3. Combine beaten eggs with cold water and stir well to blend.
4. Dip fillets first in flour, then in egg-water mixture and then in bread crumbs.
5. Fry in vegetable oil in a preheated 350° F deep fryer or electric skillet for approximately 5 to 7 minutes or until golden brown and fish is cooked throughout. Turn if necessary to ensure even browning on both sides.
6. Drain on a wire rack or paper towels.
7. Serve with cocktail or tartar sauce.
8. Garnish with a lemon wedge.

SALMON LOAF

Salmon, cooked, drained and cleaned — ½" flake	3 cups or 2 — 15½ oz. cans
Celery, ¼" dice	2 cups
Onion, ¼" dice	2 cups
Oleo Margarine	6 tablespoons
Salt	To Taste
White Pepper	½ teaspoon
Paprika	¾ teaspoon
Live Bread Crumbs	¾ cup
Eggs, large — beaten	5 each
YIELD:	6 to 8 servings

salmon loaf

PREPARATION:
1. Sauté diced celery and onion in oleo margarine until tender but not brown.
2. Add salt, white pepper and paprika to the sautéed vegetables.
3. Combine salmon, live bread crumbs and sautéed vegetables.
4. Add eggs to the salmon mixture.

5. Grease a 9¼″ x 5¼″ x 2¾″ loaf pan and line the bottom with parchment or waxed paper.
6. Place salmon mixture in loaf pan and press to edges and corners of pan.
7. Place loaf on a second baking pan with about 1″ of water in the bottom of the pan.
8. Bake in a preheated 350°F oven, approximately 60 to 75 minutes, until a knife inserted in the center comes out clean. If loaf browns too quickly, cover loosely with aluminum foil.
9. Allow a loaf to set for approximately 8 minutes, then invert onto a cutting board or serving plate.
10. Serve Salmon Loaf with Creamed Pea Sauce:
    − Prepare Cream Sauce according to instructions on recipe.
    − Measure 2 cups of cream sauce.
    − Add ½ to ¾ cup of thawed, drained peas to cream sauce. Stir to blend well.
    − Top each portion of Salmon Loaf with approximately 3 tablespoons of Creamed Pea Sauce.
11. Garnish as desired.

CRAB CAKES

Crabmeat, regular	*2 cups*
Onions, ¼″ dice	*¾ cup*
Celery, ¼″ dice	*1 cup*
Green Pepper, ¼″ dice	*2 tablespoons*
Oleo Margarine	*4 tablespoons*
Salt	*½ teaspoon*
White Pepper	*¼ teaspoon*
Mustard, prepared	*1 teaspoon*
Worcestershire Sauce	*1 teaspoon*
Mayonnaise	*¼ cup + 1 tablespoon*
Live Bread Crumbs (with crusts removed)	*1¼ cups + As Needed for Breading*
Egg, large − beaten	*2 each*
Pimiento, ¼″ dice	*1 tablespoon*
YIELD:	*6 to 8 servings*

PREPARATION:
1. Pick over crabmeat to remove any particles of shell, taking care not to break crabmeat more than is necessary.
2. Sauté diced onions, celery and green pepper in oleo margarine until tender, but not brown. Add to crabmeat.
3. Mix together salt, white pepper, prepared mustard, Worcestershire sauce and mayonnaise. Add to crabmeat.
4. Add remaining ingredients: 1¼ cups of bread crumbs, beaten eggs and diced pimiento.
5. Divide mixture into 16 equal portions. Flatten into cakes. Crab Cakes should be approximately 2½ to 3″ in diameter.
6. Dip in additional bread crumbs.
7. Fry breaded Crab Cakes in vegetable oil in a preheated 350°F fryer or electric skillet until golden brown or until Crab Cakes are cooked throughout.
8. Drain on a wire rack or paper towels.
9. Serve with tartar sauce.
10. Garnish each portion with a lemon twist.

CRABMEAT STUFFED TOMATO WITH WELSH RAREBIT SAUCE

Tomato, whole	*1 each*
Crabmeat Mixture (for crab cakes)	*½ cup*
Welsh Rarebit Sauce	*¼ cup*
Bread Crumbs, buttered	*1 teaspoon*
YIELD:	*1 serving*

PREPARATION:

1. Prepare Welsh Rarebit Sauce according to instructions given on the recipe.
2. Remove stem and core from tomato.
3. Cut tomato in quarters — cutting only ¾ of the way through to the stem end. Spread slightly to open tomato without breaking through bottom.
4. Place Welsh Rarebit Sauce in an oval casserole dish.
5. Place opened tomato on top of sauce.
6. Place crabmeat mixture on top of tomato.
7. Sprinkle crabmeat mixture with buttered bread crumbs.
8. Bake in a preheated 350° F oven for approximately 30 minutes or until heated throughout.

SHRIMP AND SEAFOOD AU GRATIN

Oleo Margarine	3 tablespoons + 1 teaspoon
Flour, all purpose	½ cup
Milk	3⅓ cups
Salt	½ teaspoon
White Pepper	¼ teaspoon + ⅛ teaspoon
Sherry Wine	3 tablespoons + 1 teaspoon
Parmesan Cheese	2 tablespoons
Cheddar Cheese, shredded	2⅞ cups
Paprika	As Needed
Shrimp, cooked, peeled and deveined	⅓ cup
Fish, cooked and flaked — 1" pieces	2 cups
Scallops, cooked	1½ cups
YIELD:	6 to 8 servings

PREPARATION:
1. Melt oleo margarine. Add flour and stir until thoroughly combined and mixture begins to bubble.
2. Add milk and continue cooking, stirring constantly until mixture begins to thicken.
3. Add salt, white pepper, parmesan and ⅞ cup of shredded cheese. Stir until cheese has completely melted.
4. Remove from heat and add sherry wine. Stir to combine.
5. Gently fold cooked shrimp, fish and scallops into Au Gratin Sauce and portion evenly into individual ramekins or casserole dishes.
6. Sprinkle remaining shredded cheese evenly on top of individual seafood au gratin casseroles. Sprinkle lightly with paprika.
7. Place ramekins or casseroles in a pan filled to the depth of 1″ water.
8. Bake in a preheated 350°F oven until heated thoroughly and cheese is melted.

SHRIMP AND SCALLOP CREOLE

Oleo Margarine	*4 tablespoons*
Shrimp, raw, cleaned — ½″ pieces	*2½ cups*
Scallops, raw — ½″ pieces	*1 cup*
Creole Sauce, heated	*4 cups*
YIELD:	*6 to 8 servings*

PREPARATION:
1. Sauté shrimp and scallops in oleo margarine until tender.
2. Combine sautéed shrimp and scallops with the heated creole sauce.
3. Serve creole over rice or toast points.
4. Garnish as desired.

SHRIMP NEWBURG

Shrimp, cooked — ¾" pieces	*2½ cups*
Onion, finely chopped	*2 tablespoons*
Mushrooms, ¼" slice	*1 cup*
Oleo Margarine	*9 tablespoons + 2 teaspoons*
Flour, all purpose	*⅔ cup*
Milk	*4 cups*
Salt	*To Taste*
White Pepper	*To Taste*
Paprika	*¾ teaspoon*
Lemon Juice, fresh	*1 tablespoon*
Parmesan Cheese	*¼ cup*
Sherry Wine	*⅜ cup*
YIELD:	*6 to 8 servings*

PREPARATION:
1. Sauté shrimp, onions and mushrooms in 4 tablespoons of oleo margarine just until vegetables are tender. Do not brown.
2. Melt remaining 5 tablespoons plus 2 teaspoons of oleo margarine. Add flour and stir until thoroughly combined and mixture begins to bubble.
3. Add milk and continue cooking, stirring constantly until mixture begins to thicken.
4. Add salt, white pepper, paprika and lemon juice to mixture.
5. Gently fold shrimp into sauce and cook over low heat until shrimp is thoroughly heated.
6. Remove from heat and add parmesan cheese and sherry wine.
7. Serve Shrimp Newburg over rice or as desired.
8. Garnish each portion with lemon slice and parsley.

FRENCH FRIED SHRIMP

PREPARATION:
1. Clean the shrimp, leaving the tail intact.
2. Split shrimp ¾ way to the tail.
3. Remove the sandbag by washing in a pan of water.
4. Soak the cleaned shrimp in a mixture of 1 tablespoon of salt dissolved in 1 cup of milk for approximately one half hour.
5. Remove from milk; drain and dip in flour — do not dip the tail.
6. Prepare egg wash: combine 2 beaten eggs with ½ cup of cold water.
7. Dip the shrimp in egg wash and then in live bread crumbs — do not dip the tail.
8. Fry breaded shrimp in vegetable oil in a preheated 350°F fryer or electric skillet until golden brown or until shrimp is cooked throughout.
9. Drain on wire rack or paper towels.
10. Serve with cocktail sauce.
11. Garnish each portion with a parsley sprig and a lemon wedge, or as desired.

Note: Soaking shrimp in the milk mixture will remove the brine flavor and allow the delicate flavor of the shrimps to become more enhanced.

SHRIMP WRAPPED IN BACON

Shrimp, breaded — uncooked	*36 to 48 each*
Bacon, raw	*18 to 24 slices*
YIELD:	*6 to 8 servings*

PREPARATION:
1. Prepare breaded shrimp according to instructions on recipe.
2. Cut bacon slices in half and wrap one half slice loosely around each breaded shrimp.
3. Pierce bacon with a toothpick to hold.
4. Fry shrimp wrapped in bacon in vegetable oil in a preheated 350°F deep fat fryer or electric skillet until bacon is crisp and shrimp is golden brown and cooked throughout.
5. Drain on wire rack or paper towels.
6. Remove toothpicks carefully from shrimp before serving.
7. Serve with cocktail or tartar sauce.
8. Garnish each portion with a parsley sprig and a lemon wedge or as desired.

SEAFOOD QUICHE

Scallops, ½" dice	*½ cup*
Shrimp, ½" dice	*½ cup*
Celery, ¼" dice	*¼ cup*
Onion, ¼" dice	*¼ cup*
Oleo Margarine	*2 tablespoons*
Eggs, large—beaten	*2 each*
Mayonnaise	*½ cup*
Milk	*½ cup*
Cornstarch	*1 tablespoon*
Chili Sauce	*2 tablespoons*
Cayenne Pepper	*⅛ teaspoon*
Salt	*½ teaspoon*
Swiss Cheese, shredded	*2 cups*
Flounder, cooked, drained and flaked—1" pieces	*½ cup*
Pie Shell with Rim (10" diameter)—unbaked	*1 each*

YIELD: *6 servings*

PREPARATION:

1. Sauté scallops, shrimp, celery and onions in oleo margarine just until cooked. Drain off all excess juices.
2. Combine beaten eggs, mayonnaise, milk, cornstarch, chili sauce, cayenne pepper and salt. Blend well.
3. Add grated Swiss cheese, flounder and scallop mixture. Blend carefully. Cover and keep refrigerated until time of use.
4. Stir mixture to combine and place in the unbaked 10" diameter pie shell.
5. Place quiche on a cookie sheet or baking tray and bake in a preheated 400°F oven for 35 to 40 minutes or until a knife inserted in the center comes out clean.
6. Allow quiche to set approximately 8 minutes before cutting.
7. Cut each 10" quiche into 6 equal wedges.
8. Garnish as desired.

SCALLOPS NORFOLK

Scallops, blanched	*¾ cup*
Butter, clarified	*2 tablespoons*
Salt	*To Taste*
White Pepper	*To Taste*
Vinegar, cider	*1 tablespoon*

YIELD: *1 serving*

PREPARATION:
1. Clarify butter:
   - Place butter in a small skillet to melt.
   - When butter is melted, carefully pour off the melted butter; discard the milky sediment in the bottom of the pan. Do not strain the melted butter.
2. Blanch scallops by placing in a metal container and dipping in boiling water for 1 minute. Immediately rinse scallops under cold running water; drain and remove small muscle on the side.
3. Heat clarified butter in a sauce pan; add blanched scallops.
4. Season lightly with salt and white pepper to taste and sauté until scallops are heated throughout.
5. Sprinkle scallops with cider vinegar and transfer to a hot, small metal casserole dish.
6. Garnish with a parsley sprig and a lemon wedge.

French Fried Onion Rings

VEGETABLES

During our many decades as a family restaurant, we've learned a very helpful lesson about vegetables—make them fun, especially for children. In that spirit, we aired television advertisements featuring animated vegetables which sang "Hot Shoppes, Hot Shoppes, all around the town." We also specialized in fun vegetables, such as french fries and onion rings.

Our Onion Rings have enjoyed a very loyal following in the Washington area; in 1980, the *Washingtonian Magazine*'s readers chose us as their favorite in the annual "The Best and Worst of Washington" poll. If those same Washingtonians are now among our readers, they'll learn why these rings are so good—a double rinsing in the egg wash, first to coat with flour and then, after a setting period, to coat with Live Bread Crumbs. It's more elaborate than other recipes, we admit...but then again, other recipes don't win magazine competitions.

Hot Shoppes' other Breaded Fried Vegetables (Zucchini and Eggplant) are also a great way to cultivate in youngsters a taste for vegetables...especially since most children no longer subscribe to the Popeye-and-spinach mythology of an earlier generation. Moreover, these recipes require that you use fresh vegetables, for which there is no substitute. That also explains why our former produce buyer used to show up daily, around 3 A.M., at the produce market at 4th and Florida Avenue in Northeast Washington. He knew that fresh vegetables fry crisper and healthier than any frozen preparation (frozen products release water when they cook, so they dilute your frying mix.). In short, only fresh vegetables can be truly animated.

FRENCH FRIED ONION RINGS

PREPARATION:
1. Use only large (at least 3" in diameter) round Spanish onions for rings.
2. Remove the solid root at the end.
3. Cut ¼" slice from the end of each onion and peel.
4. Slice onions ¼" thick and separate into rings. A full onion ring, broken on one side may be used.
5. Prepare egg wash: Combine 2 large beaten eggs with ½ cup of cold water.
6. Dip sliced onions, a few at a time, in egg wash, then dip in flour. Let flour-coated rings stand on parchment or waxed paper-lined trays in slightly overlapping rows to dry—for a minimum of 15 minutes.
7. Dip flour-coated rings again to into egg wash and then into live bread crumbs (see recipe for preparation instructions).
8. If onion rings are not fried immediately, place rings on a clean parchment or waxed paper-lined tray in slightly overlapping rows.
9. Hold refrigerated until time of service.
10. In vegetable oil, preheated to 350°F fry onion rings until golden brown. Separate onions rings during frying process to prevent them from sticking together.
11. Place only one layer of onion rings at a time in a deep fat fryer or deep electric skillet.
12. Drain on paper towels or wire racks.
13. Salt lightly before serving.

Note: Do not cover onion rings when they have been prebreaded and refrigerated. They will become soggy.

FRENCH FRIED VEGETABLES
(Zucchini, Eggplant, Cauliflower)

Use any or all of the following:
- *Fresh Zucchini*
  - Slice crosswise into ⅛" thick slices.
  - Sprinkle slices with salt and white pepper to taste and allow to stand 5 minutes.
- *Fresh Eggplant*
  - Peel eggplant and cut in half crosswise.
  - Cut each half into ⅜" thick slices.
  - Restack slices and cut into ⅜" sticks about 2 to 2½" long.
  - Season with salt and white pepper to taste.
- *Frozen Cauliflower*
  - Thaw cauliflower overnight under refrigeration.
  - Drain well and season with salt and pepper to taste.

PREPARATION:
1. Dredge vegetables well with flour; shake off excess flour.
2. Prepare egg wash: combine 2 large beaten eggs with ½ cup of cold water.
3. Dip flour-coated vegetables in egg wash.
4. Dip in live bread crumbs and place in single layers on parchment or waxed paper-lined trays.
5. Fry in vegetable shortening in a preheated 350° F deep fryer or electric skillet until golden brown and tender. Do not fry too far in advance of service.
6. Drain on wire rack or paper towels.

SOUTHERN GREEN BEANS (With Salt Pork)

Salt Pork, diced ¼ "	¼ cup
Water	2 cups
Salt (to taste)	¼ teaspoon
White Pepper	⅛ teaspoon
Green Beans—frozen, canned, or fresh cut into 1" lengths	4 cups (approx. 16 oz.)
YIELD:	4-6 servings

PREPARATION:
1. Trim rind off of salt pork. Dice into ¼ " pieces and place in a two quart sauce pan.
2. Add 1½ cups of water, salt and white pepper. Cover tightly and bring to a boil.
3. Reduce heat and simmer approximately 30 minutes or until salt pork is tender and most of the water is evaporated.
4. Add the remaining ½ cup of water and green beans. Cover tightly.
5. Return to a boil. Reduce heat and simmer until green beans are tender.

NOTE:
— If canned green beans are used, drain, and rinse with cold water before cooking with salt pork. DO NOT OVERCOOK.

CREAMED OR CAULIFLOWER AU GRATIN

Cauliflower, florets — washed	*2 quarts*
Water, cold	*1 cup*
Salt	*¾ teaspoon*
Thin Cream Sauce	*2 cups*
YIELD:	*6 to 8 servings*

PREPARATION:
1. Place cauliflower in a large sauce pan.
2. Dissolve salt in water and pour over cauliflower.
3. Bring to a boil; cover, reduce heat and simmer *just* until tender.
4. Drain thoroughly and add thin cream sauce. Stir gently to combine.

NOTE:
— For Cauliflower Au Gratin, substitute thin cheese sauce for cream sauce.

RATATOUILLE

Salad Oil	*3 tablespoons*
Onion, ½" dice	*1½ cups*
Garlic, minced	*⅜ teaspoon*
Green Pepper, ¼" x 1½" Julienne strips	*1 cup*
Zucchini, 1" dice	*2 cups*
Eggplant, 1" dice	*4 cups*
Tomatoes, canned, drained and quartered	*1 cup*
Juice from Canned Tomatoes	*6 tablespoons*
Parlsey, finely chopped	*2 tablespoons*
Thyme	*¼ teaspoon*
Basil	*½ teaspoon*
Bay Leaf	*1 each*
Salt	*To Taste*
White Pepper	*To Taste*
YIELD:	*6 to 8 servings*

PREPARATION:
1. Place salad oil in a large skillet. Add onion, garlic and green pepper and cook over low heat uncovered for approximately 15 minutes.
2. Add zucchini, eggplant, diced tomatoes, tomato juice, chopped parsley, thyme, basil, bay leaf and salt and pepper to taste.
3. Cover and simmer 15 minutes or until vegetables are tender, but not soft or mushy.
4. Remove bay leaf and serve as desired.

CORN PUDDING

Corn, whole kernel—frozen	*4½ cups*
Thin Cream Sauce	*1½ cups*
Eggs, large—beaten	*5 each*
Sugar, granulated	*⅓ cup + 1 teaspoon*
Salt	*1 teaspoon*
White Pepper	*⅛ teaspoon*
Oleo Margarine, melted	*6 tablespoons*
YIELD:	*6 to 8 servings*

PREPARATION:
1. Remove corn from freezer and allow to thaw.
2. Prepare thin cream sauce according to instructions given on the recipe.
3. Add sugar to beaten eggs and mix until sugar is completely dissolved.
4. Add salt, white pepper and cream sauce to corn; then add melted oleo margarine.
5. Add beaten eggs to mixture and blend well.
6. Place mixture in a well greased baking pan.
7. Place baking pan in a second baking pan with about 1″ of water in the bottom of the pan.
8. Bake in a preheated 350°F oven, approximately one hour or until a knife inserted in the center comes out clean.

BAKED ACORN SQUASH

Acorn Squash	*2 to 3 each*
Water, cold	*1 cup*

SUGAR MIXTURE:

Oleo Margarine	*7 tablespoons*
Sugar, granulated	*1 cup*
Orange Rind, grated	*½ teaspoon*
Orange Juice	*2 tablespoons*

YIELD: *6 to 8 servings*

PREPARATION:
1. Wash squash. Drain and cut into portions as desired.
2. Remove seeds.
3. Place portioned squash in a greased baking pan. Add water to the baking pan.
4. Cover tightly with aluminum foil and bake in a preheated 325° F oven for approximately 40 to 50 minutes, just until squash is tender. DO NOT OVERCOOK.
5. Prepare Sugar Mixture:
   — Combine all ingredients and cream together until soft and fluffy.
6. Remove aluminum foil; drain off all of the water and spread 1 to 2 tablespoons of sugar mixture inside each portion of squash, depending on the size of each individual portion.
7. Return squash to oven and continue baking, uncovered, until sugar mixture melts and flavors mellow, approximately 15 to 20 minutes.

RED CABBAGE — BAVARIAN STYLE

Bacon, raw — ½" dice	*2½ strips*
Onions, ¼" dice	*½ cup*
Vinegar, cider	*½ cup*
Sugar, granulated	*½ cup*
Salt	*1 teaspoon*
Salad Apples, large — peeled, ¼" dice	*2½ cups*
Red Cabbage, ⅛" shred	*3 quarts*
Water, hot	*4 cups*
YIELD:	*6 to 8 servings*

PREPARATION:
1. Sauté bacon and onions until golden brown.
2. Add vinegar, sugar, salt, diced apples and shredded cabbage to onion mixture and combine with hot water.
3. Cover lightly and simmer slowly at least one hour; longer cooking improves flavor.

Note: If necessary, additional water, should be added in small amounts at intervals during cooking. Do not let cabbage become dry.

ZUCCHINI ITALIAN STYLE

Onion, ¼" dice	*1 cup*
Oleo Margarine	*2 tablespoons*
Zucchini, ¼" slice	*4 cups*
Tomatoes, canned	*1 cup*
Salt	*To Taste*
White Pepper	*To Taste*
Sharp Cheddar Cheese, grated	*⅓ cup*
YIELD:	*6 to 8 servings*

PREPARATION:
1. Sauté onions in oleo margarine; add zucchini and continue cooking approximately 5 minutes. Stir frequently so that zucchini cooks evenly.
2. Dice tomatoes into ½" pieces and add with juice to squash mixture.
3. Season with salt and white pepper.
4. Place in a well greased baking pan and sprinkle with grated cheese.
5. Bake in a preheated 375°F oven until tender and slightly brown, approximately 20 minutes.

Zucchini Ilatian style

ESCALLOPED TOMATOES AND CELERY

Tomatoes, canned	*1 – 28 oz. can*
Celery, ¼" dice	*2 cups*
Onions, ¼" dice	*⅓ cup*
Oleo Margarine	*3 tablespoons + 1 teaspoon*
Salt	*To Taste*
White Pepper	*⅜ teaspoon*
Sugar, granulated	*½ tablespoon + 1 teaspoon*
White Bread, toasted	*1½ slices*

YIELD: *6 to 8 servings*

PREPARATION:
1. Drain tomatoes, reserving juice.
2. Dice tomatoes into approximate 1" pieces.
3. Sauté celery and onions in oleo margarine until tender, but not brown.
4. Combine tomatoes, juice, sautéed celery and onions, salt, white pepper and sugar. Stir to combine.
5. Place mixture in a greased baking pan or casserole dish.
6. Cut toast into ½" cubes and sprinkle on top of tomato mixture.
7. Bake in a preheated 350°F oven until hot and bubbling, approximately 30 minutes.

HOT SPICED BEETS

Onions, ⅛" slice	*½ cup*
Celery, ⅛" slice	*½ cup*
Sliced Beets, canned	*1–16 oz. can*
Vinegar, cider	*¼ cup*
Sugar, granulated	*2 tablespoons*
Bay Leaf	*½ each*
Salt	*To Taste*
White Pepper	*To Taste*
YIELD:	*4 to 6 servings*

PREPARATION:
1. Cut onion slices into quarters.
2. Drain beets, reserving juice.
3. Add vinegar, sugar, ½ bay leaf, salt and white pepper to reserved beet juice and boil for 3 minutes.
4. Remove from heat. Add thinly sliced celery and onion to hot juice.
5. Add sliced beets. Let stand until beets have absorbed flavor from seasoned juice, approximately 30 minutes.
6. Reheat and serve as desired.

Note: Remove bay leaf prior to service.

LYONNAISE POTATOES

Potatoes, peeled and shredded	*4 medium potatoes*
Onion, ¼" dice	*½ cup*
Oleo Margarine	*4 teaspoons*
Salt	*To Taste*
White Pepper	*To Taste*
YIELD:	*6 to 8 servings*

PREPARATION:
1. Sauté onion in 2 teaspoons of oleo margarine; add salt and white pepper to sautéed onions and mix well.
2. Combine seasoned sautéed onions with shredded potatoes.
3. Melt 2 teaspoons of oleo margarine in a frying pan or an electric skillet; add seasoned potatoes.
4. Flatten to approximately ¼″ thickness and press well with a spatula.
5. Fry until golden brown on one side; turn and fry second side until golden brown, adding additional oleo margarine while cooking if necessary.

OVEN BROWNED POTATOES

Potatoes, canned	2 – 16 oz. cans
Vegetable Oil	2 tablespoons
Salt	½ teaspoon
White Pepper	¼ teaspoon
Paprika	½ teaspoon
YIELD:	6 to 8 servings

PREPARATION:
1. Place potatoes in a colander and wash with cold water. Drain thoroughly.
2. Combine vegetable oil, salt, white pepper and paprika. Stir to blend well.
3. Roll each drained potato in the oil/seasoning mixture.
4. Place potatoes on a cookie sheet or in a baking pan.
5. Bake in a preheated 400° F oven until lightly browned and heated thoroughly, approximately 20 minutes.

GLAZED SWEET POTATOES

Sweet Potatoes, canned	1 – 23 oz. can
Juice from Potatoes	¼ cup
Sugar, granulated	½ cup + 1½ teaspoons
Oleo Margarine	2 tablespoons
YIELD:	6 to 8 servings

PREPARATION:
1. Drain sweet potatoes, reserving juice. Measure to ¼ cup.
2. Combine measured juice, sugar and oleo margarine and bring to a boil; simmer for 5 minutes or until mixture reaches a syrup consistency.
3. Cut potatoes in half lengthwise and place in a greased baking pan or casserole.
4. Pour hot syrup over sweet potatoes.
5. Cover with aluminum foil and bake in a preheated 350° F oven until potatoes are hot and most of the syrup flavor has been absorbed, approximately 45 minutes.

SAUTÉED OR SMOTHERED ONIONS

Onions, peeled — ¼ " slice	*1 cup*
Oleo Margarine	*1 tablespoon*
Salt	*To Taste*
YIELD:	*¾ cup*

PREPARATION:
1. Cut onion slices into quarters.
2. Sauté onions in oleo margarine until tender, but not brown. Stir frequently to prevent excess browning or burning. Onions should be slightly crisp when done.
3. Serve as an accompaniment or garnish with entrees.

RICE PILAU

Rice, raw	*1 cup + 2 tablespoons*
Oleo Margarine	*8 tablespoons*
Onions, ¼ " dice	*1 cup*
Chicken Stock	*3½ cups*
White Pepper	*To Taste*
Raisins, seedless	*3 tablespoons*
Water, warm	*As Needed*
Toasted Almonds, ¼ " chop	*1 tablespoon*
YIELD:	*6 to 8 servings*

PREPARATION:
1. Melt oleo margarine and add raw rice. Cook approximately 8 minutes, stirring frequently.
2. Add diced onions and continue cooking for approximately 2 minutes.
3. Add chicken stock and white pepper.
4. Pour mixture into a greased baking dish or casserole. Cover tightly with aluminum foil.
5. Bake in a preheated 325°F oven until tender and liquid is absorbed, approximately 45 minutes.
6. Cover raisins with warm water. Soak for half an hour and drain well.
7. Combine drained raisins and chopped toasted almonds with rice and mix gently until ingredients are evenly distributed.
8. Serve as desired.

SPANISH RICE

Rice, raw	¾ cup
Oleo Margarine	4 tablespoons
Onion, ¼" dice	½ cup
Green Pepper, ¼" dice	½ cup
Tomatoes, canned — ½" dice with juice	1⅔ cups
Salt	To Taste
White Pepper	To Taste
Poultry Seasoning	¼ teaspoon
Chicken Stock	1⅔ cups
YIELD:	6 to 8 servings

PREPARATION:
1. Wash rice in cold water and drain thoroughly.
2. Melt oleo margarine in a medium size frying pan; add raw rice.
3. Cook over moderate heat approximately 5 minutes, stirring constantly.
4. Add diced onion and green peppers and continue cooking an additional 5 minutes.
5. Add diced tomatoes and juice, salt, white pepper and poultry seasoning and chicken stock. Stir well to blend.
6. Place in a well greased casserole or baking dish.
7. Cover tightly with aluminum foil.
8. Bake in a preheated 350°F oven for approximately 45 to 60 minutes or until the rice is tender and the stock is absorbed.

Hot Fudge Ice Cream Cake

DESSERTS, DESSERT SAUCES

All food should look good, of course, but for some reason, diners are particularly keen about the appearance of their desserts. Perhaps it's because desserts appear alone, as opposed to entrees, which usually are served on the same plate with vegetables. In any case, we've developed desserts that look good. And because the Hot Shoppes also served drive-in diners, we've had to create desserts that travel well, that quite literally, are well balanced. You will note that our instructions for the Hot Fudge Ice Cream Cake call for you to pour the hot fudge only over the corners of the ice cream cake. If by mistake you cover the cake with fudge, then your whip cream will slide off the top (LBJ's younger daughter, Luci Baines, enjoyed this dessert twice-a-week during her father's presidency, always with the whip cream in its proper place).

A second feature of our desserts is that they encourage frugality and efficiency. If, for instance, you've finished shopping for dinner but have neglected to make special arrangements for dessert, you'll find recipes here that call for ingredients you're likely to have on hand. Raisin Rice Custard and Bread and Butter Pudding fall into this category.

The Strawberry Glaze also deserves special notice, because it is one of our earliest and most sought after recipes.

HOT FUDGE ICE CREAM CAKE

Plain Yellow Cake, day old—3" x 3" x ½"	*2 slices*
Ice Cream Square, 3" x 3"	*1 each*
Hot Fudge, heated	*4 tablespoons*
Whipped Cream	*2½ tablespoons*
Maraschino Cherry, half–drained	*1 each*
YIELD:	*1 serving*

PREPARATION:
1. Place 1 square of plain yellow cake on serving plate.
2. Top with the ice cream square and place the second square of plain yellow cake on top of the ice cream.
3. Drizzle 1 tablespoon of hot fudge over each of the four cake corners, taking care to leave the center of the cake free from fudge.
4. Place approximately 2½ tablespoons of whipped cream in the top center of the cake square. If desired, use a pastry bag to pipe whipped cream onto top of cake in a rosette shape.
5. Top center of whipped cream with a well drained maraschino cherry half to garnish.

FRUIT DELIGHT

CAKE MIXTURE	
Flour, all purpose	*¾ cup + 2 tablespoons*
Sugar, granulated	*½ cup + 1 tablespoon*
Baking Powder, double acting	*1⅛ teaspoons*
Salt	*⅛ teaspoon*
Oleo Margarine	*4 tablespoons*
Milk	*¼ cup*
Vanilla Extract	*½ teaspoon*
Eggs, large	*2 each*
Fruit Filling: Cherry, Peach or Blackberry, heated	*3½ cups*
YIELD:	*6 to 8 servings*

PREPARATION:
1. Sift together flour, sugar, baking powder and salt in a medium size mixing bowl.
2. Combine oleo margarine with flour mixture and mix until ingredients are completely blended.
3. Combine milk and vanilla extract; add slowly to the mix.

4. Continue beating approximately 4 minutes.
5. Add eggs one at a time, mixing well after each addition. Scrape bowl frequently to ensure that all ingredients are well blended.
6. Place heated fruit filling in a greased 8″ x 8″ baking pan.
7. Carefully pour batter over the entire surface of the heated fruit mixture.
8. Bake in a preheated 325° F oven for approximately 40 minutes or until a toothpick inserted in the center comes out clean. If cake browns too quickly, cover with aluminum foil.
9. Serve as desired, slightly warm or at room temperature.

BROWNIES (With Glace Frosting)

Sugar, granulated	*1⅞ cups*
Oleo Margarine	*¾ cup + 2 tablespoons + 1 teaspoon*
Eggs, large	*3 each*
Flour, cake	*1¾ cups*
Milk	*2½ tablespoons*
Salt	*¼ teaspoon*
Bittersweet Chocolate, melted	*2¾ –1 oz. bars*
Pecans, finely chopped	*⅔ cup*

GLACE FROSTING

Sugar, Confectioners	*1¾ cup*
Corn Syrup	*1 teaspoon*
Water, hot	*3 tablespoons*
Bittersweet Chocolate	*2–1 oz. bars*
Oleo Margarine	*½ tablespoon*
Vanilla Extract	*½ teaspoon*

YIELD: *1–9″ x 13″ x 2″ pan*

PREPARATION:
1. Cream sugar and oleo margarine until smooth, scraping bowl once or twice.
2. Add flour, salt, milk and eggs and beat until creamy.
3. Add melted chocolate and chopped pecans. Mix until well blended.
4. Spread brownie batter evenly in a greased and floured 9″ x 13″ x 2″ baking pan.
5. Bake in a preheated 300° F oven for approximately 35 to 40 minutes or until a toothpick inserted in the center comes out clean.
6. Remove brownies from oven. Cool on a wire rack.

7. PREPARE GLACE FROSTING:
   - Dissolve the corn syrup in hot water.
   - Sift the confectioners sugar and add the hot water/corn syrup mixture.
   - Melt the chocolate and oleo margarine together; combine with the sugar mixture. Stir to combine.
   - Add vanilla extract and continue stirring until all ingredients are thoroughly combined.
8. Frost brownies with Glace Frosting.
9. Cut and serve as desired.

Note: If frosting becomes too heavy before it is used, stand bowl or pan in hot water and stir to spreading consistency. Do not melt, just warm.

APPLE DUMPLINGS

Baking Apples — peeled and cored	*6 each*
Pastry Dough	*Double Recipe*
Oleo Margarine, melted	*4 tablespoons*
Sugar, granulated	*¾ cup*
Nutmeg, ground	*¼ teaspoon*
Cinnamon, ground	*¼ teaspoon*
YIELD:	*6 servings*

PREPARATION:
1. Combine sugar, nutmeg and cinnamon. Blend well.
2. Roll pastry dough ⅛″ thick.
3. Cut pastry dough into squares large enough to cover each entire apple, approximately 8″ x 8″.

Apple dumpling with cinnamon Sauce

4. Place 1 apple in the center of each pastry square and top with 2 tablespoons of the sugar mixture and 1 teaspoon of melted oleo margarine.
5. Moisten edges of pastry with water and bring each corner to center and seal pastry at the top only. Leave sides open.
6. Brush dumpling pastry with melted oleo margarine.
7. Place apple dumplings in an ungreased baking pan and bake in a preheated 375°F oven for 45 to 60 minutes or until pastry is browned and apples are done.
8. Serve Apple Dumplings warm with Cinnamon Sauce, whipped cream or vanilla ice cream as desired.

WARM APPLE CHEESE CRISP

Apples, baking—peeled, cored	*6 each (Approximately 7 cups)*
Sugar, granulated	*1¼ cups*
Cinnamon, ground	*¾ teaspoon*
Salt	*½ teaspoon*
Flour, all purpose	*⅔ cup + ¼ cup*
Sharp Cheddar Cheese, grated	*1¾ cups*
Oleo Margarine, room temperature	*8 tablespoons*
YIELD:	*6 to 8 servings*

PREPARATION:
1. Thinly slice each apple.
2. Place sliced apples in a well greased 6½″ x 10½″ baking dish.
3. Combine sugar, cinnamon, salt, flour and grated sharp cheddar cheese. Do not use a mixer.
4. Work room temperature oleo margarine into flour mixture to make a crumbly topping. Work *just* until it begins to stick together.
5. Spread the flour mixture on top of the apple slices. Cover with aluminum foil and place baking dish in a preheated 350°F oven. Bake for 25 minutes to cook apples.
6. Remove foil from baking dish. Return crisp to oven and continue baking until crumbs turn brown.
7. Serve Apple Cheese Crisp warm topped with vanilla ice cream or as desired.

RAISIN RICE CUSTARD PUDDING

Eggs, large	*5 each*
Sugar, granulated	*½ cup*
Milk	*3½ cups*
Salt	*⅜ teaspoon*
Rice, cooked	*1 cup*
Vanilla Extract	*1 teaspoon*
Raisins, seedless	*⅔ cup*
Nutmeg, ground	*As Needed*
YIELD:	*6 to 8 servings*

PREPARATION:
1. Beat eggs and sugar to blend thoroughly.
2. Add milk, salt, cooked rice and vanilla.
3. Wash raisins and *drain well*. Set aside.
4. Pour custard mixture into a well greased baking dish or casserole.

5. Sprinkle raisins over top of custard mixture to ensure even distribution.
6. Sprinkle top surface with nutmeg.
7. Place baking dish or casserole in a larger baking pan filled with 1″ of water.
8. Bake in a preheated 350°F over for approximately 1 hour and 15 minutes or until a knife inserted in the center comes out clean. DO NOT OVERBAKE.
9. Serve as desired, slightly warm or well chilled.

NOTE:
— If desired, additional cooked rice may be added to the recipe.

If pudding is overbaked, it will separate and become watery

BREAD AND BUTTER PUDDING

Bread	*2 slices*
Oleo Margarine, softened	*As Needed*
Eggs, large	*6 each*
Sugar, granulated	*½ cup + 2 tablespoons*
Milk	*3¾ cups*
Salt	*¼ teaspoon*
Nutmeg, ground	*¼ teaspoon*
Vanilla Extract	*1 teaspoon*
Raisins, seedless — washed and drained	*1 cup*
YIELD:	*6 to 8 servings*

PREPARATION:
1. Spread sliced bread lightly with softened oleo margarine and cut in 1″ cubes.
2. Beat eggs slightly with sugar and add milk, salt, nutmeg and vanilla.
3. Place bread cubes evenly over the bottom of well greased baking dish.
4. Pour custard mixture over bread cubes.
5. Sprinkle raisins evenly over the custard mixture.
6. Sprinkle top surface with nutmeg.
7. Place baking dish in a larger baking pan filled to a 1″ depth with water.

8. Bake in a preheated 350°F oven for approximately 1 hour and 15 minutes or until a knife inserted in the center comes out clean.
9. Serve as desired, slightly warm or well chilled.
10. Garnish with whipped cream.

TAPIOCA CREAM

Milk, cold	2¾ cups
Tapioca, minute	⅓ cup
Sugar, granulated	½ cup
Egg Yolks	3 each
Salt	Dash
Vanilla Extract	1½ teaspoons
Egg Whites	3 each
YIELD:	6 to 8 servings

PREPARATION:
1. Place tapioca in cold milk and heat in a double boiler until tapioca is clear and stays suspended on the top of the milk. Stir frequently while cooking. Scrape sides of pan with a spoon to make certain all tapioca is free from the side of the double boiler.
2. Beat egg yolks slightly and add ¼ cup of granulated sugar, stirring continuously while sugar is added.
3. Add a small amount of the hot tapioca mixture, stirring constantly.
4. Add egg yolk and tapioca mixture to the remaining hot mixture in the double boiler.
5. Continue cooking, stirring constantly—about 6 minutes until egg yolks are cooked and mixture has thickened.
6. Add salt and vanilla extract; blend well.
7. Beat egg whites and remaining ¼ cup sugar until very stiff. Add the hot tapioca *slowly* to the stiffened egg whites. Fold egg whites gently until well blended.
8. Serve as desired.
9. Garnish with a fresh mint sprig, fresh strawberries or other fresh fruit.

NOTE: Do not beat egg whites ahead of time — they will become thin and watery.

BAKED CUSTARD

Sugar, granulated	*½ cup*
Oleo Margarine, room temperature	*2 tablespoons*
Eggs, large	*6 each*
Milk	*2 cups*
Salt	*⅛ teaspoon*
Vanilla Extract	*¼ teaspoon*
Nutmeg, ground	*As Needed*
YIELD:	*6 to 8 servings*

PREPARATION:
1. Beat sugar and oleo margarine until creamy.
2. Add eggs and continue beating.
3. Add milk, salt and vanilla extract; continue beating until completely blended.
4. Place mixture into oven proof individual custard cups or ramekins.
5. Sprinkle top with nutmeg.
6. Place filled custard cups in a pan filled to 1″ with water.
7. Bake in a preheated 350°F oven for approximately 30 minutes or until a knife inserted in the center comes out clean.
8. Serve slightly warm or well chilled as desired.

STEWED PRUNES WITH LEMON

Prunes, dried	*1 pound*
Water, cold	*3 cups*
YIELD:	*6 to 8 servings*

PREPARATION:
1. Wash prunes and soak in cold water at least 5 hours.
2. Place soaked prunes and water in a baking pan or casserole dish.
3. Cover tightly and cook slowly until prunes are tender and pits remove easily.
4. Cool slightly, remove pits from prunes, then refrigerate until well chilled.
5. Serve prunes with juice in individual small dessert dishes.
6. Garnish with ½ slice of lemon twisted in the center of each portion or as desired.

CHOCOLATE BAVARIAN

Milk	1 cup
Bittersweet Chocolate	2⅓ – 1 oz. bars
Gelatin, Plain	1 tablespoon + 1 teaspoon
Water, cold	⅔ cup
Egg Yolks	6 each
Sugar, granulated	½ cup
Egg Whites	6 each
Salt	⅛ teaspoon
Whipped Topping	⅔ cup
YIELD:	6 to 8 servings

PREPARATION:
1. Heat milk and chocolate slowly over low heat.
2. Soak gelatin in cold water and add to hot milk.
3. Beat egg yolks slightly and add sugar; continue blending until thoroughly combined.
4. Mix a spoonful of hot milk with egg yolk mixture before adding to the entire hot mixture.
5. Cook until *slightly* thickened. Chill until mixture is cold, but not stiff or lumpy. Stir frequently while cooling.
6. Add salt to egg whites and beat until very stiff.
7. When chocolate mixture has cooled, stir to blend well, then gradually fold chocolate mixture into beaten egg whites.
8. Fold whipped topping gently into the mixture.
9. Portion mixture into 3 or 4 ounce individual molds and refrigerate until completely set.
10. Unmold each portion onto serving plate.
11. Garnish with whipped topping and top with shaved chocolate, maraschino cherry half or fresh mint sprig.

Note: Do not beat egg whites ahead of time - they will become thin and watery

COCONUT SNOWBALL SUNDAE

Vanilla Ice Cream, hard frozen	1 or 2 scoops
	(Approximately 2½ tablespoons for each scoop)
Coconut, moist	As Needed
Hot Fudge, heated	2 tablespoons
YIELD:	1 serving

PREPARATION:
1. Place hot fudge sauce in the bottom of a serving dish.
2. Roll hard ice cream scoops in coconut until well covered and appearance resembles a "snowball."
3. Place ice cream coconut balls on top of hot fudge.
4. Garnish as desired.

NOTE: Coconut balls may be made ahead and held in freezer. Remove from freezer as needed in small quantities just before serving.

SOFT CUSTARD SAUCE

Milk, cold	*2 cups*
Flour, all purpose	*1 tablespoon*
Sugar, granulated	*4 tablespoons*
Egg Yolks	*3 each*
Salt	*⅛ teaspoon*
Vanilla Extract	*½ teaspoon*

YIELD: *2 cups*

PREPARATION:
1. Heat 1½ cups of milk to boiling in the top half of a double boiler.
2. Blend flour and 2 tablespoons of sugar together. Add the remaining ½ cup of cold milk and blend well.
3. Add the cold mixture to the boiling milk, stirring until the mixture thickens.
4. Beat egg yolks slightly and add the remaining 2 tablespoons of sugar. Blend well with yolks.
5. Add *some* of the thickened flour, sugar, milk mixture to the yolk/sugar mixture, stirring constantly and return mixture to the double boiler.
6. Continue heating, stirring constantly until eggs are *just* cooked and mixture coats a spoon when stirred. Do not overcook or mixture will separate.
7. Remove from heat; add vanilla and blend well.
8. Pour mixture into a shallow dish or bowl and refrigerate until time of service.
9. Serve as a dessert sauce.

RUM SAUCE

Sugar, dark brown	*⅓ cup*
Sugar, granulated	*½ cup*
Oleo Margarine	*8 tablespoons*
Half and Half	*½ cup*
Rum Extract	*¼ teaspoon*
YIELD:	*1½ cups*

PREPARATION:
1. Melt oleo margarine in the top half of a double boiler. Add dark brown and granulated sugars.
2. Stir in half and half and continue cooking until mixture thickens, approximately 20 minutes.
3. Add rum extract and stir thoroughly to combine.
4. Serve warm as a dessert sauce.

LEMON SAUCE

Sugar, granulated	*1¾ cups*
Cornstarch	*2 tablespoons*
Salt	*¼ teaspoon*
Water, boiling	*1⅔ cups*
Egg Yolks — beaten	*2 each*
Lemon Juice, fresh	*2 tablespoons + 2 teaspoons*
Lemon Rind, grated	*½ tablespoon*
Oleo Margarine	*1 tablespoon + 2 teaspoons*
YIELD:	*2 cups*

PREPARATION:
1. Mix sugar, cornstarch and salt until thoroughly combined.
2. Add mixture slowly to boiling water, stirring constantly while blending.
3. Cook approximately 15 minutes, stirring constantly to prevent lumping. Remove from heat.
4. Add beaten egg yolks, stirring constantly while adding.
5. Add lemon juice, lemon rind and oleo margarine. Blend well.
6. Serve warm as a dessert sauce.

CINNAMON SAUCE

Sugar, granulated	*½ cup*
Apple Juice	*¾ cup*
Cornstarch	*1 tablespoon*
Water, cold	*¾ cup*
Cinnamon, ground	*1 teaspoon*
Nutmeg, ground	*¼ teaspoon*
Oleo Margarine	*1 tablespoon + 1 teaspoon*
YIELD:	*1½ cups*

PREPARATION:
1. Place ¼ cup of sugar, apple juice and ½ cup of water in a medium size sauce pan. Bring mixture to a boil.
2. In a small mixing bowl, add cornstarch to cold water and mix thoroughly until completely dissolved.
3. Add cornstarch solution to boiling juice and cook over low heat until mixture thickens and becomes clear, approximately 10 minutes, stirring frequently.
4. Mix cinnamon and nutmeg with the remaining ¼ cup of sugar; add to sauce and stir until completely blended.
5. Add oleo margarine to mixture and stir until oleo margarine has melted and is completely blended into sauce.
6. Serve sauce warm with apple dumplings or as desired.

STRAWBERRY GLAZE

Strawberries, fresh — cleaned and stemmed	*1½ cups*
Water, cold	*¾ cup*
Sugar, granulated	*1 cup*
Cornstarch	*4 tablespoons + 1 teaspoon*
Red Food Coloring	*Optional*
YIELD:	*1½ cups*

PREPARATION:
1. In a 2 quart sauce pan, combine 1½ cups of strawberries — thinly sliced *or* crushed. Stir in ½ cup water and simmer until berries are very soft, about 10 minutes.
2. Strain mixture through a wire mesh strainer, pushing most of pulp through.
3. Add sugar to the juice and bring to a boil.
4. Add cornstarch to the remaining ¼ cup of *cold* water and stir to dissolve.
5. Slowly add the cornstarch water to the boiling juice and cook over low heat until thick and clear, approximately 5 minutes.
6. Add optional red food coloring to obtain desired color.
7. Remove glaze from heat and allow to cool slightly.
8. Use glaze warm when preparing Fresh Strawberry Pie or serve as a topping for Cheesecake or other desserts.

PINEAPPLE SAUCE

Pineapple Juice	*2⅓ cups*
Sugar, granulated	*⅓ cup*
Salt	*Dash*
Cornstarch	*2 tablespoons*
Oleo Margarine	*2 tablespoons*
YIELD:	*2 cups*

PREPARATION:
1. Combine 2 cups of pineapple juice, sugar and salt. Bring to a boil.
2. Dissolve cornstarch in remaining ⅓ cup of pineapple juice; add to boiling juice.
3. Add oleo margarine and continue cooking until mixture thickens and becomes clear.
4. Serve warm over Pineapple Upside Down Cake or as desired.

Oatmeal Cake with Cranberry, Banana and Nut Topping

CAKES, FROSTINGS

Over the years, the Hot Shoppes have served their cakes on a rotating schedule, which has also created a rotating demand. So every one of our cooks has to be capable of preparing every one of these dishes on short notice, for those rare occasions when the Commissary truck is delayed. They're not especially difficult, so even inexperienced cooks will be able to produce first-rate cake…provided their ovens are properly calibrated.

The Icebox Cheese Cake is among the simpler and quicker recipes — so much so, that for many years it was made at every one of the Hot Shoppes, without creating too much of an extra burden for the extremely busy cooks.

In recent years, health conscious Americans have expressed a desire for desserts featuring grains, nuts and fruits. The Oatmeal Cake with Cranberry, Banana and Nut Topping has been an especially successful answer to their requests. If however, you aren't counting calories too carefully, consider using one of our frostings on your favorite cake. The Hot Shoppe's Buttercream Frosting recipe can be easily converted to Lemon, Cherry, Mocha, Orange, Pineapple, and Chocolate Buttercream, and therefore adapts to a whole range of desserts.

OATMEAL CAKE WITH CRANBERRY, BANANA, AND NUT TOPPING

CAKE BATTER
Quick Oats	*1 cup*
Water, boiling	*1 cup*
Oleo Margarine	*½ cup*
Sugar, brown	*1¼ cups*
Sugar, granulated	*½ cup + 2 tablespoons*
Eggs, large	*3 each*
Flour, all purpose	*1¾ cups*
Cinnamon, ground	*1 teaspoon*
Baking Soda	*1 teaspoon*
Vanilla Extract	*1 teaspoon*

TOPPING
Sugar, granulated	*⅔ cup*
Cranberries, fresh—finely chopped	*1 cup*
Bananas, peeled—⅛" dice	*3 each*
Pecans, finely chopped	*½ cup*

YIELD: *8 to 12 servings*

PREPARATION:
1. Place quick oats in a bowl. Pour boiling water over quick oats, stir and let stand until water is absorbed and mixture cools to room temperature.
2. Combine oleo margarine, sugars, and eggs. Cream on low speed of electric mix for approximately 5 minutes or until all ingredients are thoroughly combined.
3. Mix flour, cinnamon, baking soda, vanilla extract and quick oats together. Add to oleo margarine mixture and blend on low speed for 2 minutes.
4. Pour mixture into a greased and floured 13" x 9" x 2" baking pan.
5. Prepare topping:
   − Combine sugar, cranberries, bananas and nuts. Blend well.
6. Sprinkle topping evenly over oatmeal cake batter.
7. Bake in a preheated 350°F oven for approximately 40 to 45 minutes or until a toothpick inserted in the center comes out clean.
8. Remove from oven and cool on a wire rack.
9. Garnish each portion with a rosette of whipped cream and a fresh cranberry or as desired.

DATE NUT TORTE

Eggs, large	10 each
Sugar, brown	2 cups
Dates, ¼" cut	1½ cups
Flour, all purpose	2 tablespoons
Baking Powder, double acting	2 tablespoons + 2 teaspoons
Cake Crumbs, (white or yellow) day old, crumbled	4 cups
Vanilla Extract	1½ teaspoons
Nuts, finely chopped	1½ cups
YIELD:	8 to 12 servings

PREPARATION:
1. Beat eggs until thick and lemon colored.
2. Add sugar slowly, beating continuously.
4. Add dates and nuts.
5. Mix baking powder with crumbs and add to egg and date mixture.
6. Add vanilla extract and pour into a greased and floured 13" x 9" x 2" baking pan.
7. Bake in a preheated 325°F oven for approximately 40 to 50 minutes or until a toothpick inserted in the center comes out clean.
8. Cool on a wire rack.
9. Garnish with whipped cream or dessert sauce as desired.

Note: Cut dates with wet scissors into ¼" pieces and dust lightly with the two tablespoons of flour before adding to the mixture.

ROMAN APPLE CAKE

CAKE MIXTURE

Sugar, brown	*⅔ cup*
Sugar, granulated	*½ cup + 1 tablespoon*
Oleo Margarine	*½ cup + 2 tablespoons*
Eggs, large	*2 each*
Flour, cake	*3¼ cups*
Salt	*1 teaspoon*
Nutmeg, ground	*1 teaspoon*
Cinnamon, ground	*1 teaspoon*
Baking Powder, double acting	*¾ teaspoon*
Baking Soda	*2 teaspoons*
Buttermilk	*½ cup*
Apples—peeled, cored and	*3¼ cups finely chopped*

TOPPING

Oleo Margarine	*5 tablespoons*
Sugar, granulated	*¾ cup*
Cinnamon, ground	*1¼ teaspoons*
Flour, all purpose	*3 tablespoons*
Almonds, sliced	*⅔ cup*

YIELD:	*8 to 12 servings*

PREPARATION:
1. Cream sugars with oleo margarine.
2. Add eggs one at a time, beating until light.
3. Sift flour with nutmeg, cinnamon, salt, baking powder and soda.
4. Add flour mixture alternately with buttermilk to the creamed mixture. Mix *just* enough to blend.
5. Add finely chopped apples, mixing just enough to blend.
6. Prepare topping:
   - Blend oleo margarine, sugar, cinnamon and flour until mixture begins to stick together when pressed.
7. Pour batter into a greased and floured 13″ x 9″ x 2″ baking pan.
8. Crumble topping and spread evenly over cake mixture.
9. Sprinkle evenly with sliced almonds.

10. Bake in a preheated 350°F oven for approximately 55 to 60 minutes or until a toothpick inserted in the center comes out clean. DO NOT OVERBAKE.
11. Cool on a wire rack.
12. Garnish with whipped cream or as desired.

Note: If cake browns too quickly before it has completely baked, cover loosely with aluminum foil during the last few minutes of baking.

PINEAPPLE UPSIDE DOWN CAKE

CAKE BATTER

Flour, all purpose	*2 cups*
Sugar, granulated	*1⅓ cups*
Baking Powder, double acting	*3½ teaspoons*
Salt	*¾ teaspoon*
Oleo Margarine	*½ cup + 1 tablespoons*
Milk	*1 cup*
Vanilla Extract	*1½ teaspoons*
Eggs, large	*2 each*

TOPPING

Oleo Margarine	*5 tablespoons + 1 teaspoon*
Sugar, brown	*1⅓ cups*
Pineapple Rings — drained, reserve juice	*12 each*
Maraschino Cherries — drained and cut in half	*6 each*

YIELD:	*12 servings*

PREPARATION:
1. Sift together flour, sugar, baking powder and salt in a medium size mixing bowl.
2. Add oleo margarine and continue mixing until well combined.
3. Combine milk and vanilla extract and add to the flour mixture in a slow, steady stream.
4. Continue mixing for approximately 4 minutes. Scrape down bowl twice during mixing to ensure that all ingredients are well blended.
5. Add eggs one at a time, beating ½ minute after each addition. Scrape down bowl after each egg is added.
6. Grease a 13″ x 9″ x 2″ baking pan.

7. Prepare topping:
   — Melt oleo margarine. Add brown sugar and stir until mixture is very smooth and free from lumps.
   — Spread mixture evenly in the bottom of the greased baking pan.
   — Arrange pineapple rings over topping mixture.
   — Place a maraschino cherry half, cut side up in each ring so that the rounded side is up when the cake is turned upside down.
8. Pour cake batter carefully into the prepared baking pan, spreading evenly over topping.
9. Bake in a preheated 350° F oven for approximately 35 minutes or until a toothpick inserted in the center comes out clean.
10. Invert cake immediately onto a serving tray and let cool at least 30 minutes before serving to allow topping to firm up.
11. Serve cake slightly warm topped with warm Pineapple Sauce.

GINGERBREAD

Sugar, granulated	*½ cup*
Oleo Margarine	*5 tablespoons*
Egg, large	*1 each*
Light Molasses	*½ cup*
Baking Soda	*1 teaspoon*
Baking Powder, double acting	*1 teaspoon*
Buttermilk	*¾ cup*
Flour, all purpose	*1¼ cups*
Cinnamon, ground	*½ tablespoon*
Nutmeg, ground	*1 teaspoon*
Allspice, ground	*½ teaspoon*
Ginger, ground	*½ teaspoon*
YIELD:	*6 to 8 servings*

PREPARATION:
1. Sift flour with spices, soda and baking powder.
2. Cream together oleo margarine and sugar.
3. Add the egg slowly, beating continuously while adding.
4. Add half of the flour mixture and mix thoroughly.
5. Add half of the buttermilk to the mixture. Scrape sides of mixing bowl to ensure that all ingredients are thoroughly combined.
6. Add the remaining flour and buttermilk and the molasses last. Mix until smooth and all ingredients are thoroughly combined.
7. Pour batter into a greased and floured 8″ x 8″ x 2″ baking pan.

8. Bake in a preheated 325°F oven for approximately 30 minutes or until a toothpick inserted in the center comes out clean.
9. Serve Gingerbread warm or at room temperature, as desired.
10. Garnish with one of the following or as desired:
    — Top with Lemon or Soft Custard Sauce.
    — Top with a rosette of whipped cream.
    — Top with applesauce, whipped cream and chopped nuts.

ICE BOX CHEESE CAKE

CAKE BATTER

Gelatin, plain	*2 tablespoons*
Water, cold	*1 cup*
Egg Yolks	*4 each*
Egg Whites	*4 each*
Sugar, granulated	*½ cup*
Cream Cheese, softened	*2 cups (16 oz.)*
Orange Juice	*3 tablespoons*
Orange Rind, grated	*2 tablespoons*
Salt	*½ teaspoon*
Heavy Cream	*1 cup*

CRUMB CRUST

Yellow Cake, day old	*4 cups*
Sugar, granulated	*2 tablespoons + 1 teaspoon*
Oleo Margarine, melted	*5 tablespoons*
YIELD:	*8 to 10 servings*

PREPARATION:
1. Soak gelatin in cold water.
2. Combine egg yolks and ¼ cup of sugar in the top half of a double boiler.
3. Heat egg yolks and sugar until slightly thickened.
4. Add soaked gelatin to the yolk and sugar mixture. Stir until completely blended. Remove from heat and cool.
5. Beat together softened cream cheese, orange juice, orange rind and salt until light and fluffy.
6. Add cooled egg mixture to the cheese mixture and stir until thoroughly combined.
7. Beat egg whites and remaining ¼ cup of sugar until stiff.
8. Add cheese mixture slowly to the beaten egg whites, folding *carefully* until well combined.
9. Whip heavy cream and fold into mixture.

10. Prepare crumb crust:
    — Break up cake by hand until mealy in appearance.
    — Add sugar and *melted* oleo margarine and blend well.
    — Place crumbs in a 13″ x 9″ x 2″ pan and press to the bottom to form a crust.
11. Spread cheese cake batter mixture carefully over the pressed crumb crust. Refrigerate until set.
12. Garnish as desired.

BUTTERCREAM FROSTING

Sugar, confectioners	*3½ cups*
Oleo Margarine	*6 tablespoons*
Half and Half	*¼ cup*
Vanilla Extract	*1 teaspoon*
Corn Syrup	*2 teaspoons*
YIELD:	*2 cups*

PREPARATION:
1. Sift the confectioners sugar.
2. Cream sugar with oleo margarine; add half and half slowly and continue creaming until light and fluffy.
3. Add vanilla extract and corn syrup. Continue mixing until frosting is of a spreading consistency, scraping the bowl once or twice during mixing to ensure that all ingredients are thoroughly blended.
4. Frost cake between the layers, then frost sides — and last of all the top.
5. If desired, finely chopped nuts may be pressed against the sides of the cake to garnish.

VARIATIONS:
Lemon Frosting: — omit the vanilla extract and add ⅛ cup of fresh lemon juice and 1 teaspoon of grated lemon rind.
Cherry Frosting — add 2 tablespoons of finely chopped and well drained maraschino cherries.
Mocha Frosting — omit the vanilla extract and add 2 teaspoons of instant coffee and ⅓ oz. of melted bittersweet chocolate.
Orange Frosting — omit vanilla extract and add ⅛ cup of orange juice, fresh or reconstituted and 1 teaspoon of grated orange rind.
Pineapple Frosting — omit vanilla extract and add ⅓ cup of crushed pineapple, well drained.

CHOCOLATE BUTTERCREAM FROSTING

Buttercream Frosting	1 recipe (2 cups)
Chocolate, bittersweet	4 – 1 oz. bars

YIELD: 2¼ cups

PREPARATION:
1. Melt chocolate in the top half of a double boiler. Cool
2. Prepare Buttercream Frosting according to instructions given on recipe.
3. Add cooled chocolate to Buttercream Frosting and stir until thoroughly blended.
4. Frost cake between the layers, then frost sides—and last of all the top.

Note: If necessary add additional cream for frosting to become of spreading consistency.

Fresh Strawberry Pie

PIES, PASTRIES

Having already informed you that our cakes are relatively simple to prepare makes it a bit easier for us to advise you that our pies are relatively complicated. The recipe for Pie Crust Dough alone is one of the longer sets of instructions, and the crust, of course is a prerequisite for all of these items.

Like our cakes, our pies have usually been offered on a rotating basis, except for Apple Pie, which has achieved such enthusiastic response that it is usually featured daily at most Hot Shoppes.

The Fresh Strawberry Pie has been as popular as the Apple Pie down through the years. Our original recipe took almost two years to perfect, with a great many testings in the taste kitchen. The recipe we've included here captures the best of that long process.

The most important element in getting it right has always been the strawberries: each must be fresh, so check the cap to see that it's green, and make certain that the skin is intact. If the leaves are browning and wilted, or if there's any evidence of mold or other damage to the skin, you should discard it. And after picking your strawberries, be certain to wash them before slicing off their caps. If you wash them after slicing, you run the risk of rinsing sand or straw into their cores.

FRESH STRAWBERRY PIE

Fresh Strawberries	1½ quarts
Strawberry Glaze	1½ cups
Pie Shell, baked — 9" deep dish or 10" diameter	1 each
Whipped Cream, optional	To Garnish
YIELD:	1 pie — 6 servings

PREPARATION:
1. Wash strawberries one pint at a time (to prevent mashing) by floating in a bowl of water. To prevent bruising of berries, do not rinse under faucet and do not allow berries to soak in water.
2. Drain berries by placing them in a single layer on paper towel-lined trays.
3. Remove stems and any bruised areas. Cut very large strawberries in half.
4. Prepare Strawberry Glaze:

Fresh Strawberries — cleaned and stemmed	1½ cups
Cold Water	¾ cup
Sugar, granulated	1 cup
Cornstarch	4 tablespoons + 1 teaspoon
Red Food Coloring	Optional
YIELD:	1½ cups

In a 2 quart saucepan, combine 1½ cups strawberries — thinly sliced or crushed. Stir in ½ cup water and simmer until berries are very soft, about 10 minutes. Strain mixture through a wire mesh strainer, pushing most of pulp through. Add sugar to the juice and bring to a boil. Add cornstarch to the remaining ¼ cup of cold water and stir to dissolve. Slowly add the cornstarch water to the boiling juice and cook over low heat until thick and clear, approximately 5 minutes. Add optional red food coloring to obtain desired color. Remove glaze from heat and allow to cool slightly. Use glaze warm when preparing pie.

5. In a medium mixing bowl combine the 1½ quarts of cleaned, stemmed strawberries and 1½ cups of Strawberry Glaze. Stir gently with a rubber spatula to coat all berries with glaze.
6. Pour berry mixture into a baked pie shell, distributing evenly with a mound of berries toward center of shell.
7. Refrigerate pie about 1½ hours to set glaze before cutting. For optimum quality, the pie should be served within several hours of preparation.
8. Cut pie into six equal wedges.
9. Garnish each portion with whipped cream, if desired.

APPLE PIE

Apples, baking—peeled, cored and thinly sliced	*5 to 6 cups (Approx. 6 to 7 apples)*
Sugar, granulated	*¾ to 1 cup*
Flour, all purpose	*2 tablespoons*
Salt	*Dash*
Cinnamon, ground	*½ to 1 teaspoon*
Nutmeg, ground	*¼ teaspoon*
Oleo Margarine or Butter, firm—cut in small pieces	*2 tablespoons*
Pie Crust Dough	*1 recipe (double crust)*

YIELD: *6 to 8 servings*

PREPARATION:
1. Prepare pie crust dough according to instructions given on recipe. Line a 9″ deep dish or a 10″ diameter pie plate with pastry.
2. Combine sugar, flour, salt, cinnamon and nutmeg until thoroughly blended; mix with thinly sliced apples until all apples are coated evenly.
3. Fill crust-lined pie plate with apple mixture. Dot filling with oleo margarine or butter pieces. Wet rim of pastry with a small amount of cold water.
4. Position top crust over apple filling with approximately 1″ of dough extended over the rim of the pan.
5. Press top and bottom crust together well to seal.
6. Fold top crust under bottom crust along the edge of the pie and flute edges.
7. Slash top crust with your own design or prick with a fork to allow steam to escape during baking.
8. Place pie on a baking tray or cookie sheet and bake in a preheated 400°F oven for approximately 45 to 50 minutes until pie is golden brown and apples are tender.
9. Remove pie from oven and allow to cool on a wire rack for 2 to 3 hours before cutting.
10. If desired, sprinkle top surface of pie with a cinnamon sugar mixture immediately upon removal from oven.
11. Cut pie in 6 to 8 wedges and serve with vanilla ice cream, if desired.

PEACHY PECAN PIE

Sugar, granulated	*1 tablespoon*
Oleo Margarine	*1 tablespoon + 2 teaspoons*
Flour, all purpose	*3 tablespoons*
Corn Syrup	*1¾ cups*
Salt	*Dash*
Vanilla Extract	*1 teaspoon*
Eggs, large	*4 each*
Pecans, finely chopped	*¾ cup*
Peaches, canned and drained — ½" dice	*⅓ cup*
Pie Crust Dough	*1 each single crust*

YIELD: *6 to 8 servings*

PREPARATION:
1. Prepare pie crust dough according to instructions on recipe. Line a 9" deep dish or 10" diameter pie plate with crust, extending crust approximately ½" to 1" beyond the edge of the plate. Fold crust under and flute edges.
2. Cream sugar and oleo margarine until light.
3. Add flour, syrup, salt and vanilla.
4. Beat eggs until foamy and add to creamed mixture and continue mixing for approximately 2 minutes until all ingredients are thoroughly combined.
5. Place finely chopped pecans in pie shell. Top with liquid mixture.
6. Sprinkle well drained diced peaches on top of pie.
7. Place pie on a baking tray or cookie sheet.
8. Preheat oven to 400°F. Reduce temperature to 325°F.
9. Bake pie in preheated oven at 325°F for approximately 50 to 55 minutes *just* until filling mixture is set and crust is golden brown. Overbaking will result in pie filling "weeping."
10. Remove pie from oven and allow to cool completely on a wire rack before serving.
11. Cut pie in 6 to 8 wedges and serve with vanilla ice cream or garnish each portion with a rosette of whipped cream or as desired.

SOUTHERN ALMOND PIE

Sugar, granulated	⅓ cup + 2 tablespoons
Almond Paste	2 tablespoons + 1 teaspoon
Oleo Margarine	4 tablespoons + 2 teaspoons
Flour, all purpose	¼ cup
Corn Syrup	1⅜ cups
Eggs, large	5 each
Almond Extract	1 teaspoon
Salt	Dash
Almonds, sliced	½ cup + 2 tablespoons
Pie Crust Dough	1 each single crust
YIELD:	6 to 8 servings

Southern almond pie

PREPARATION:
1. Prepare pie crust dough according to instructions on recipe. Line a 9″ deep dish or a 10″ diameter pie plate with crust, extending crust approximately ½″ to 1″ beyond the edge of the plate. Fold crust under and flute edges.
2. Cream together sugar, almond paste and oleo margarine until smooth. Hold remaining almond paste in a tightly closed jar or container after it has been opened.
3. Add flour and corn syrup and mix well.
4. In a separate mixing bowl, beat eggs until light and lemon colored, approximately 2 minutes.
5. Add eggs slowly to the first mixture; then add almond extract and salt.
6. Pour mixture into fluted pie shell.
7. Sprinkle sliced almonds evenly over pie filling.
8. Place pie on a baking tray or cookie sheet and bake in a preheated 350°F oven for approximately 50 to 60 minutes until crust is golden brown and filling mixture is set. Do not allow pie to puff completely in center or crack before removing from oven.
9. Remove pie from oven and allow to cool completely on a wire rack before serving.
10. Cut pie in 6 to 8 wedges and garnish each portion with a rosette of whipped cream, or as desired.

COCONUT CUSTARD PIE

Sugar, granulated	½ cup
Oleo Margarine, room temperature	2 tablespoons
Eggs, large	6 each
Milk	2 cups
Salt	⅛ teaspoon
Coconut, flaked	½ cup + 2 tablespoons
Nutmeg, ground	As Needed
Pie Crust Dough	1 each single crust
Oleo Margarine, melted	½ tablespoon
YIELD:	6 to 8 servings

PREPARATION:
1. Prepare pie crust dough according to instructions on recipe. Line a 9″ deep dish or a 10″ diameter pie plate with crust, extending crust approximately ½″ to 1″ beyond the edge of the plate. Fold crust under and flute edges. *Brush raw pie shell with ½ tablespoon oleo margarine and refrigerate.*
2. Beat together sugar and oleo margarine until creamy.
3. Add eggs, one at a time and continue beating until mixture is well blended.
4. Add milk; then salt and vanilla. Continue mixing until ingredients are thoroughly combined.
5. Place coconut in the bottom of the refrigerated pie shell.
6. Carefully pour custard filling on top of coconut.
7. Dust top of pie lightly with nutmeg.
8. Place pie on a baking tray or cookie sheet and bake in a preheated 400°F oven for 15 minutes until the crust is well set.
9. Reduce oven temperature to 350°F and continue baking for approximately 50 to 60 minutes until the custard has puffed around the edge, but still has a small indentation in the center or until a knife inserted in the center comes out clean.
10. Remove pie from oven and allow to cool completely on a wire rack before serving.
11. Cut pie into 6 to 8 wedges.

NOTE:
— For Custard Pie, omit flaked coconut as an ingredient.

Custard pies should be held under refrigeration.

SWEET POTATO PIE

Sweet Potatoes, canned and drained	2 cups
Sugar, granulated	1 cup
Nutmeg, ground	¾ teaspoon
Oleo Margarine	5 tablespoons + 1 teaspoon
Eggs, large	2 each
Milk, evaporated	¾ cup
Pie Crust Dough	1 each single crust

YIELD: 6 to 8 servings

PREPARATION:
1. Prepare Pie Crust Dough according to instructions on recipe. Line a 9" deep dish or a 10" diameter pie plate with crust, extending crust approximately ½" to 1" beyond the edge of the plate. Fold crust under and flute edges.
2. Place sweet potatoes in a medium size mixing bowl. Using an electric mixer, beat until all lumps are removed and texture is smooth.
3. Sift together sugar and nutmeg. Cream sugar mixture with oleo margarine until all ingredients are thoroughly combined.
4. Add eggs and continue beating. Scrape bowl and beaters to ensure that all ingredients are mixed well.
5. Add potatoes and evaporated milk last. Mix until well blended.
6. Pour filling into pie shell.
7. Place pie on a baking tray or cookie sheet and bake in a preheated 400°F oven for approximately 50 to 60 minutes until mixture is set and slightly browned. Do not let pie completely puff on top or crack. Bottom crust must be done.
8. Remove pie from oven and allow to cool completely on a wire rack before serving.
9. Cut pie into 6 to 8 wedges and garnish each portion with a rosette of whipped cream, or as desired.

NOTE:
— Custard type pies should be held under refrigeration.

LEMON MERINGUE PIE

FILLING

Water, cold	*1⅔ cups + ½ cup*
Sugar, granulated	*¾ cup + ⅓ cup*
Cornstarch	*¼ cup*
Egg Yolk, large	*4 each*
Lemon Juice, fresh	*¼ cup + 1 tablespoon*
Lemon Extract	*¾ teaspoon*
Yellow Food Coloring	*Optional*
Salt	*⅛ teaspoon*
Pie Shell, baked—9" deep dish or 10" diameter	*1 each single crust*

MERINGUE

Egg Whites, large	*4 each*
Sugar, granulated	*¼ cup*
Cream of Tartar	*¼ teaspoon*
Cornstarch	*1½ teaspoons*
Water, cold	*1 tablespoon + 1 teaspoon*

YIELD:	*6 to 8 servings*

PREPARATION:

1. Prepare pie shell dough according to instructions given on recipe. Line a pie plate with crust, extending crust approximately ½" to 1" beyond the edge of the pie plate. Fold crust under and flute edges. Prick bottom and sides of crust with a fork. This will prevent puffing as the shell bakes. Bake in a preheated 450°F oven until pastry is golden brown, approximately 10 to 12 minutes. Remove pie shell from oven and allow to cool completely on a wire rack.
2. Bring 1⅔ cups of water and ¾ cup of sugar to a boil in the top half of a double boiler.
3. Dissolve cornstarch in remaining ½ cup of cold water and add slowly to the boiling water and sugar, stirring constantly while adding. Cook until mixture is thick and clear.
4. Beat egg yolks slightly; add remaining ⅓ cup sugar and mix well.
5. Add a small amount of the hot mixture to the yolk/sugar mixture; return to the hot mixture. Bring to a boil over high heat, stirring constantly. Reduce heat to low; cook and stir approximately 4 minutes until egg yolks are completely cooked.
6. Add oleo margarine, lemon juice, lemon extract and salt. Stir until oleo margarine is completely melted.
7. Remove filling from heat. Cover entire surface with clear plastic wrap. Set aside and let cool for 10 minutes.

8. Prepare meringue:
   - Place egg whites, sugar and cream of tartar in a medium size mixing bowl.
   - Dissolve cornstarch in the cold water and add to the egg/sugar mixture.
   - Beat until stiff and glossy, but not dry. To test, place a knife in the beaten meringue, then strike the knife on the edge of the bowl. If meringue leaves the knife clean it is beaten enough for use.
9. Pour slightly cooled filling into prebaked pie shell.
10. Place meringue on top of slightly cooled filling, spreading well to seal meringue to edges of pastry shell all around. This prevents shrinking.
11. Bake in a preheated 300°F oven for approximately 30 minutes or until meringue is an even light brown in color.
12. Remove pie from oven and allow to cool completely before serving.
13. Cut pie into 6 to 8 wedges.

NOTE:
— Beat meringue to have ready at the same time the filling has cooled for 10 minutes.
— If a deeper yellow color is desired for the filling, yellow food coloring may be added to the filling one drop at a time until the desired color is achieved.

Beat meringue before filling pie shell.

STRAWBERRY CHIFFON PIE

Strawberries, thawed with juice	*1⅛ cups*
Strawberry Juice, reserved	*3 tablespoons*
Gelatin, plain	*4 teaspoons*
Egg Yolks, large	*4 each*
Sugar, granulated	*½ cup + ⅓ cup*
Red Food Coloring	*Optional*
Egg Whites, large	*4 each*
Salt	*⅛ teaspoon*
Pie Shell, baked—9" deep dish or 10" diameter	*1 each single crust*
YIELD:	*6 to 8 servings*

PREPARATION:

1. Prepare pie crust dough according to instructions given on recipe. Line a pie plate with crust, extending crust approximately ½″ to 1″ beyond the edge of the pie plate. Fold crust under and flute edges. Prick bottom and sides of crust with a fork. This will prevent puffing as the shell bakes. Bake in a preheated 450°F oven until pastry is golden brown, approximately 10 to 12 minutes. Remove pie shell from oven and allow to cool completely on a wire rack.
2. Drain off measured amount of juice from strawberries.
3. Sprinkle gelatin on *cold* strawberry juice. Stir to dissolve.
4. Beat egg yolks slightly; add ½ cup sugar and blend well.
5. Heat egg yolk mixture in the top half of a double boiler until egg thickens. Stir constantly.
6. Add dissolved gelatin to hot egg mixture. Stir until completely blended. Remove from heat.
7. Add strawberries and remaining juice and optional red food coloring. Blend well.
8. Refrigerate and cool mixture *just* until it begins to thicken. *Do not* allow to gel.
9. Add remaining ⅓ cup of sugar to egg whites. Beat until stiff and glossy, but not dry. Whites are beaten enough when a knife inserted in beaten whites comes out clean when struck on the edge of the bowl.
10. Fold the chilled strawberry mixture into the beaten whites. Fold in *gently* by hand. *Do not* over mix.
11. Pour filling into prebaked pie shell.
12. Refrigerate until filling is set, approximately 2 to 3 hours.
13. Top pie with approximately 1½ cups of stiffly whipped cream or whipped topping. Spread evenly over top surface of pie, leaving the whipped cream surface rough on top.
14. Cut pie into 6 to 8 wedges. Garnish each portion with a fresh strawberry slice or as desired.

NOTE:
— Beat egg whites when the cooked mixture is almost ready.

If gelatin cooks when added to the egg mixture, it will not congeal.

PASTRY DOUGH

Flour, all purpose	*2 cups*
Baking Powder, double acting	*1 tablespoon + 1 teaspoon*
Baking Soda	*¼ teaspoon*
Salt	*⅛ teaspoon*
Shortening, firm	*⅔ cup*
Buttermilk	*½ cup*
YIELD:	*2—9" or 10" diameter crusts*

PREPARATION:
1. Sift together flour, baking powder, soda and salt.
2. Blend firm shortening with the flour mixture until mealy with pieces the size of small peas.
3. Add buttermilk *all at once*. Mix lightly, just enough to blend well.
4. Shape dough into a ball.
5. On a *lightly* floured surface, flatten dough ball slightly and roll ⅛" thick. If edges split while rolling, pinch them together.
6. Use as directed on individual recipes or as desired.

NOTE:
— Dough should be mixed in small batches for best results.
— Use as little flour as possible to roll dough.
— Always roll dough in a spoke-like fashion, going from the center to the edge of the dough.

Dough should be mixed in small batches for best results.

PIE CRUST DOUGH

Shortening, firm	*1 cup + 2 tablespoons*
Flour, all purpose	*2⅓ cups*
Salt	*½ teaspoon*
Water, ice cold	*6 tablespoons*
YIELD:	*2—9" or 10" diameter crusts*

PREPARATION:
1. Blend firm shortening with flour until mealy with pieces the size of small peas.
2. Add salt to ice cold water and stir to dissolve completely.
3. Add ice cold water *all at once*. Mix lightly, just enough to blend well. Do not overmix or hold in a hot place.
4. Shape dough into a ball. For a two crust pie, divide dough in half for top and bottom crusts or use as directed for two single crusts.
5. On a lightly floured surface, flatten dough ball slightly and roll ⅛" thick. If edges split while rolling, pinch them together.
6. Transfer pastry to pie plate. Fit loosely onto bottom and sides to line a 9" deep dish or 10" diameter pie plate with crust, extending crust approximately ½" to 1" beyond the edge of the pie plate.

• For a double crust pie:
— Fit the bottom crust in the pie plate. Trim bottom crust even with the rim of the pie plate; moisten the edge.
— Fill with desired filling.
— Position top crust, trimming ½" to 1" beyond the edge of the pie plate. Fold crust under to seal the edge of the bottom crust and then flute edges.
— Slash top crust with your own design or prick with a fork to allow steam to escape during baking.
— Bake as directed on individual recipes.
• For a single crust pie:
— Line a 9" deep or 10" diameter pie plate with crust, extending crust approximately ½" to 1" beyond the edge of the pie plate.
— Fold crust under and flute edges.
— Fill with desired filling and bake as directed on individual recipes.
• For a baked pie shell:
— Prick bottom and sides of crust with a fork. This will prevent puffing as the shell bakes.
— Bake in a preheated 450°F oven until golden brown, approximately 10 to 12 minutes.
— Remove pie shell from oven and allow to cool completely on a wire rack.
— Fill as directed on individual recipes.

NOTE:
— Dough should be mixed in small batches for best results.
— Use as little flour as possible to roll dough.

Always roll dough in a spoke-like fashion, going from the center to the edge of the dough.

DIRECTORY OF HOT SHOPPES

Next time you're in the greater Washington, D.C. area, you're likely to find yourself near one of these Hot Shoppes. We invite you to sample from our full range of meals, many of which you've already learned about in our cookbook.

Address	City	State
1750 Pennsylvania Avenue	Washington	District of Columbia
4287 Branch Avenue, S.E.	Temple Hills	Maryland
3500 East-West Highway	Hyattsville	Maryland
11160 Viers Mill Road	Wheaton	Maryland
5454 Wisconsin Avenue	Chevy Chase	Maryland
7101 Democracy Blvd., Montgomery Mall	Bethesda	Maryland
7500 Wisconsin Avenue	Bethesda	Maryland
7900 New Hampshire Avenue	Langley Park	Maryland
2401 Brightseat Road, Landover Mall	Landover	Maryland
1699 Rockville Pike, Congressional Plaza	Rockville	Maryland
5611 Columbia Pike	Falls Church	Virginia
6001 Columbia Pike	Falls Church	Virginia
2173 Crystal Plaza Arcade	Arlington	Virginia
Tyson's Corner Center	McLean	Virginia
6648 Springfield Mall	Springfield	Virginia
501 Jefferson Davis Highway	Fredericksburg	Virginia

Numerals in bold indicate a photograph of the subject mentioned.

A

A & W Root Beer Float 26
A & W Root Beer Float in
  Frosted Mug **24**, 26
Appetizers:
  Celery Stuffed With:
    Herb Cottage Cheese 36
    Spring Cottage Cheese 36
    Pimiento Cottage
      Cheese 36
  Chopped Chicken Livers 38
  Clam Dip 35
  Eggs:
    Deviled 37
    Stuffed 37
  Fruit Cup with Sherbet 32
  Seafood Cocktail **30**, 33
  Shrimp:
    Cocktail 35
    Cooking 34
Apple Dumplings **189**, 188
Apple Pie 213
Apple Waldorf Salad 101

B

Baked Acorn Squash 176
Baked Chicken Southern
  Style 142
Baked Custard 193
Baked Ham with Orange Raisin
  Sauce 136
Baked Stuffed Fillet of Fish 159
Banana Pecan Salad 104
Banana Muffins 68
Barbeque Country
  Spareribs 135
Barbeque Sandwiches:
  Beef 115
  Chicken 117
  Pork 116
Barbeque Sauce 87
Barbeque Slaw 95
Basic Fruit Punch 28
Beef, Macaroni and
  Tomatoes 154
Beef Stew 124
Beef Stroganoff 133
Beef Stuffed Cabbage with
  Tomato Sauce 128
Beef Stuffed Peppers with
  Tomato Sauce 125
Beef Turnover with Gravy 132
Beverages:
  A & W Root Beer Float 26
  A & W Root Beer in Frosted
    Mug 26

Basic Fruit Punch 28
Cranberry Punch 29
Lemonade with Sherbert 27
Milk Shakes:
  Chocolate 28
  Coffee 28
  Pineapple 28
  Strawberry 28
  Vanilla 28
Orange Freeze 27
Blue Cheese Dressing 108
Blueberry Muffins 68
Bran Muffins 73
Bread and Butter Pudding 191
Bread Crumbs:
  Buttered 60
  Cheese Crumb Topping 60
  Live Bread Crumbs 59
Bread Dressing 63
Breaded Veal Cutlet with
  Fricassee Sauce 134
Breads:
  Buns:
    Hot Cross Buns 57
    Rum Buns 55
  Buttermilk Biscuits 59
  Corn Bread 66
  Corn Sticks 66
  Crumbs:
    Buttered 60
    Cheese Crumb Topping 60
    Live Bread Crumbs 59
  Croutons:
    Cheese 61
    Seasoned 61
  Fricassee Dumplings 62
  Hush Puppies 65
  Muffins:
    Banana 68
    Blueberry 68
    Bran 73
    Cherry 69
    Glazed Apple Corn Bread
      Muffins 75
    Nut 67
    Pineapple 70
    Plain 67
    Pumpkin 72
    Raisin 67
    Spice 71
    Spiced Apple 74
  Rolls:
    Cheese Rolls 52
    Yeast Rolls: 53
    Cloverleaf 54
    Parker House 54
  Spoon Bread 65
Brown Gravy 89
Brownies with Glace
  Frosting 187
The Buckboard Sandwich 118

Buns:
  Hot Cross 57
  Rum 55
Buttercream Frosting 208
Buttered Crumbs 60
Buttermilk Biscuits 59

C

Cakes:
  Date Nut Torte 203
  Gingerbread 206
  Icebox Cheese Cake 207
  Oatmeal Cake with Cran-
    berry, Banana and
    Nut Topping 202
  Pineapple Upside Down
    Cake 205
  Roman Apple Cake 204
Casseroles:
  Beef, Macaroni and
    Tomatoes 154
  Cheese Souffle 149
  Chicken Pot Pie 151
  Chicken Tetrazzini 153
  Escalloped Potatoes with
    Ham 155
  Macaroni Au Gratin 148
  Monterey Jack Vegetable
    Bake 150
Celery, Apple and Nut
  Salad 105
Celery Sauce 80
Celery Stuffed with:
  Herb Cottage Cheese 36
  Pimiento Cottage Cheese 36
  Spring Cottage Cheese 36
Cheese Croutons 61
Cheese Crumb Topping 60
Cheese Rolls **50**, 52
Cheese Souffle 149
Cheese Topping for Au Gratin
  Items 60
Cherry Muffins **50**, 69
Chicken (See Poultry)
Chicken Cacciatore **145**, 144
Chicken Croquette 141
Chicken Fried Beefsteak with
  Gravy 13
Chicken Noodle Soup 39
Chicken Pot Pie **152**, 151
Chicken Salad 94
Chicken Soup with Rice 43
Chicken Tetrazzini 153
Chocolate Bavarian 194
Chocolate Buttercream
  Frosting 209
Chocolate Milkshake 28
Chopped Chicken Livers 38
Chowders: (see Soups)
  Manhattan Clam Chowder 48

New England Clam
  Chowder 47
Cinnamon Sauce 197
Clam Dip 35
Clear French Dressing 108
Clear Vegetable Soup 40
Cloverleaf Rolls 54
Cocktail Sauce 79
Coconut Custard Pie 216
Coconut Snowball Sundae 194
Coffee Milkshake 28
Cole Slaw 96
Cole Slaw Dressing 111
Corn Bread 66
Corn Bread Dressing 63
Corn Pudding 175
Corn Sticks 66
Cottage Cheese and Tomato
  Salad 98
Crab Cakes 162
Crab Cake Sandwich 119
Crabmeat Stuffed Tomato with
  Welsh Rarebit
  Sauce 163
Cranberry Punch 29
Cranberry Sauce 80
Creamed or Cauliflower Au
  Gratin 174
Creole Sauce **76**, 86
Croutons:
  Cheese 61
  Seasoned 61

D
Date Nut Torte 203
Desserts:
  Apple Dumplings 188
  Baked Custard 193
  Bread and Butter
    Pudding 191
  Brownies with Glace
    Frosting 187
  Chocolate Bavarian 194
  Coconut Snowball
    Sundae 194
  Fruit Delight 186
  Hot Fudge Ice Cream
    Cake 186
  Raisin Rice Custard
    Pudding 180
  Stewed Prunes with
    Lemon 193
  Tapioca Cream 192
  Warm Apple Cheese
    Crisp 190
Dessert Sauces:
  Cinnamon Sauce 196
  Lemon Sauce 196
  Pineapple Sauce 199

Rum Sauce 196
Soft Custard Sauce 195
Strawberry Glaze 198
Deviled Egg Salad 95
Dressing for Stuffed Fish 64
Dressings:
  Bread Dressing 63
  Cheese Topping for Au Gratin
    Items 60
  Corn Bread Dressing 63
  Dressing for Stuffed Fish 64

E
Egg and Asparagus Salad 100
Eggs:
  Deviled 37
  Stuffed 37
Enchilada Sauce 84
Escalloped Potatoes with
  Ham 155
Escalloped Tomatoes and
  Celery 179

F
Fish: (See Seafood)
  Baked Stuffed Fillet of
    Fish 159
  French Fried Fillet of
    Fish 160
  French Fried Shrimp 167
  Fried Fillet of Fish
    Almondine 158
  Salmon Loaf 161
French Fried Fillet of Fish 160
French Fried Onion
  Rings **170**, 172
French Fried Shrimp 167
French Fried Vegetables:
  Cauliflower 172
  Eggplant 172
  Zucchini 172
French Onion Soup Au
  Gratin 45
Fresh Strawberry Pie **210**, 212
Fricassee Chicken and
  Dumplings 142
Fricassee Dumplings 62
Fried Fillet of Fish
  Almondine **156**, 158
Frostings:
  Buttercream 208
  Chocolate Buttercream 209
  Fruit Cup with Sherbet 32
  Fruit Delight 186

G
Gingerbread 206
Glazed Apple Corn Bread
  Muffins **50**, 75
Glazed Sweet Potatoes 181

Gravies:
  Brown Gravy 89
  Onion Gravy 91
  Vegetable Gravy 90
Grilled Reuben 120

H
Ham and Swiss Cheese
  Quiche 137
Hamburger Royale 118
Heavenly Hash 106
Honey Yogurt Dressing (for Fruit
  Salad) 110
Horseradish Sour Cream
  Sauce 78
Hot Cross Buns 57
Hot Fudge Ice Cream
  Cake **184**, 186
Hot Potato Salad 99
Hot Sauce 81
Hot Spiced Beets 180
Hush Puppies 65

I
Icebox Cheese Cake 207
Italian Sauce 85

L
Lemon Butter 78
Lemon Meringue Pie 219
Lemon Sauce 196
Lemonade with Sherbet 27
Live Bread Crumbs 59
Lyonnaise Potatoes 180

M
Macaroni Au Gratin **146**, 148
Manhattan Clam Chowder 48
Marinated Tomato and Green
  Pepper Salad 96
Maryland Style Fried
  Chicken **138**, 140
Meats:
  Baked Ham with Orange
    Raisin Sauce 136
  Barbeque Country
    Spareribs 135
  Beef Stew 124
  Beef Stroganoff 133
  Beef Stuffed Cabbage with
    Tomato Sauce 128
  Beef Stuffed Peppers with
    Tomato Sauce 125
  Beef Turnover with Gravy 132
  Breaded Veal Cutlet with
    Fricassee Sauce 134
  Chicken Fried Beefsteak with
    Gravy 131
  Ham and Swiss Cheese
    Quiche 137

Meat Loaf 129
Meatballs in Sweet and Sour
   Sauce 126
Salisbury Steak 131
Sicilian Chopped Steak 130
Swedish Meatballs with
   Onion Gravy 127
Meatballs in Sweet and Sour
   Sauce 126
Meatless Spaghetti Sauce 85
Meatloaf 129
Medium Cheese Sauce 83
Medium Cream Sauce 82
Medium Fricassee Sauce 83
Mighty Mo Sandwich 114
Mighty Mo Sauce 79
Milk Shakes:
   Chocolate 28
   Coffee 28
   Pineapple 28
   Strawberry 28
   Vanilla 28
Molded Fruit Salad 102
Monterey Jack Vegetable
   Bake 150
Muffins:
   Banana 68
   Blueberry 68
   Bran 73
   Cherry 69
   Glazed Apple Corn Bread 75
   Nut 67
   Pineapple 70
   Plain 67
   Pumpkin 72
   Raisin 72
   Spice 74
   Spiced Apple 74

N
Navy Bean Soup 74
New England Clam
   Chowder 47
Nut Muffins 67

O
Oatmeal Cake with Cranberry,
   Banana and Nut
      Topping 200, 202
Old Fashioned Vegetable
   Soup 41
Onion Gravy 91
Orange Freeze 27
Oven Browned Potatoes 181
Oyster Bisque 49

P
Parker House Rolls 54
Pastries (See Pies)
Pastry Dough 222
Peachy Pecan Pie 214

Pearadise Salad 106
Peppercream Dressing 92, 107
Pickled Beet Salad 100
Pies:
   Apple Pie 213
   Coconut Custard Pie 216
   Fresh Strawberry Pie 212
   Lemon Meringue Pie 219
   Pastry Dough 222
   Pie Crust Dough 222
   Peachy Pecan Pie 214
   Southern Almond Pie 215
   Strawberry Chiffon Pie 220
   Sweet Potato Pie 218
Pie Crust Dough 222
Pineapple Cheese Salad 103
Pineapple Mayonnaise 110
Pineapple Milk Shake 28
Pineapple Muffins 70
Pineapple Sauce 199
Pineapple Upside Down
   Cake 205
Plain Muffins 67
Poultry:
   Baked Chicken Southern
      Style 142
   Chicken Cacciatore 144
   Chicken Croquette 141
   Fricassee Chicken and
      Dumplings 142
   Maryland Style Fried
      Chicken 140
   Sautéed Chicken Livers 143
Pumpkin Muffins 72

R
Raisin Muffins 67
Raisin Rice Custard
   Pudding 190
Ratatouille 174
Red Cabbage—Bavarian
   Style 177
Rice Pilau 182
Rice Pudding
Rolls: (See Breads)
   Cheese 52
   Yeast: 53
      Cloverleaf 54
      Parker House 34
Roman Apple Cake 204
Rum Buns 56, 55
Rum Sauce 196

S
Salads:
   Apple Waldorf Salad 101
   Banana Pecan Salad 104
   Barbeque Salad 95
   Celery, Apple and Nut
      Salad 105
   Chicken Salad 94

Cole Slaw 96
Cottage Cheese and Tomato
   Salad 98
Deviled Egg Salad 95
Egg and Asparagus
   Salad 100
Heavenly Hash 106
Hot Potato Salad 99
Marinated Tomato and Green
   Pepper Salad 96
Molded Fruit Salad 102
Pearadise Salad 100
Pineapple Cheese Salad 103
Tomato Aspic 97
Tropical Fresh Fruit
   Platter 101
Tuna Salad 94
Salad Dressings:
   Blue Cheese Dressing 108
   Clear French Dressing 108
   Cole Slaw Dressing 111
   Honey Yogurt Dressing (for
      Fruit Salads) 110
   Peppercream Dressing 107
   Pineapple Mayonnaise 110
   Yogurt Dressing (for
      Vegetable Salads) 109
Salisbury Steak 131
Salmon Loaf 161
Sandwiches:
   Barbeque Sandwiches
      Beef 115
      Chicken 117
      Pork 116
   Crab Cake Sandwich 119
   Grilled Reuben 120
   Hamburger Royale 118
   Mighty Mo 112, 114
   Steak and Cheese 121
   Talk of the Town 119
   Teen Twist 115, 114
   The Buckboard 118
Sauces:
   Barbeque Sauce 87
   Celery Sauce 80
   Cocktail Sauce 79
   Cranberry Sauce 80
   Creole Sauce 80
   Enchilada Sauce 84
   Horseradish Sour Cream
      Sauce 78
   Hot Sauce 81
   Italian Sauce 85
   Lemon Butter 78
   Meatless Spaghetti
      Sauce 85
   Medium Cheese Sauce 83
   Medium Cream Sauce 82
   Medium Fricassee Sauce 83
   Mighty Mo Sauce 79
   Savory Tomato Sauce 87

St. Louis Sauce 88
Sweet and Sour Sauce 89
Welsh Rarebit Sauce 81
Sautéed Chicken Livers 143
Sautéed or Smothered
  Onions 182
Savory Tomato Sauce 87
Scallops Norfolk 169
Seafood: (see Fish)
  Crab Cakes 162
  Crabmeat Stuffed Tomato
    with Welsh Rarebit
    Sauce 163
  Scallops Norfolk 169
  Seafood Quiche 168
  Shrimp:
    French Fried 167
    Newburg 166
    and Scallop Creole 165
    and Seafood Au Gratin 164
    Wrapped in Bacon 167
Seafood Cocktail **30**, 33
Seafood Quiche 168
Seasoned Croutons 61
Shrimp:
  Cocktail 35
  Cooking 34
  French Fried 167
  Newburg 166
  and Scallop Creole 165
  and Seafood Au Gratin 164
  Wrapped in Bacon 167
Sicilian Chopped Steak 130
Soft Custard Sauce 195
Soups:
  Chicken Noodle Soup **30**, 39
  Chicken Soup with Rice 43
  Clear Vegetable Soup 40
  French Onion Soup Au
    Gratin **45**
  Manhattan Clam Chowder 48
  Navy Bean Soup 44
  New England Clam
    Chowder 47
  Old Fashioned Vegetable
    Soup 41
  Oyster Bisque 49
  Split Pea Soup 42
Southern Almond Pie **215**
Southern Green Beans 173
Spanish Rice 183
Spice Muffins 71
Spiced Apple Muffin 74
Split Pea Soup 42
Spoon Bread 65
St. Louis Sauce 88
Steak and Cheese
  Sandwich 121
Stewed Prunes with Lemon 193

Strawberry Chiffon Pie 220
Strawberry Glaze 198
Strawberry Milk Shake 28
Swedish Meatballs with Onion
  Gravy 127
Sweet Potato Pie 218
Sweet and Sour Sauce 89

T
Talk of the Town 119
Tapioca Cream 192
Teen Twist 114
Tomato Aspic 97
Tropical Fresh Fruit Platter 101
Tuna Salad 94

V
Vanilla Milk Shake 28
Vegetables:
  Baked Acorn Squash 176
  Corn Pudding 175
  Creamed or Cauliflower Au
    Gratin 174
  Escalloped Tomatoes and
    Celery 179
  French Fried Onion
    Rings 172
  French Fried Vegetables:
    Cauliflower 172
    Eggplant 172
    Zucchini 172
  Glazed Sweet Potatoes 181
  Hot Spiced Beets 180
  Lyonnaise Potatoes 180
  Oven Browned Potatoes 181
  Ratatouille 174
  Red Cabbage—Bavarian
    Style 177
  Rice Pilau 182
  Sautéed or Smothered
    Onions 182
  Southern Green Beans 173
  Spanish Rice 183
  Zucchini Italian Style 178
Vegetable Gravy 90

W
Warm Apple Cheese Crisp 190
Welsh Rarebit Sauce 81

Y
Yeast Rolls 53
Yogurt Dressing (for Vegetable
  Salads) 109

Z
Zucchini Italian Style **178**